Table of Contents

W9-APG-996

Table of Contents *continued*

Unit 5: Capitalization and Punctuation

Unit 6: Composition

Introduction

The National Council of Teachers of English and the International Reading Association prepared standards for the English language arts. These standards "grew out of current research and theory about how students learn—in particular, how they learn language." These standards address "what students should know and be able to do in the English language arts."

One standard is that students should be able to communicate effectively by learning the "language of wider communication," the forms of the English language that are most commonly identified as standard English. Students must recognize the importance of audience when they write and speak so they will be able to use the appropriate form of language for the intended audience. The standards acknowledge that "students need guidance and practice to develop their skills in academic writing. . . . They need to understand the varying demands of different kinds of writing tasks and to recognize how to adapt tone, style, and content for the particular task at hand." Again, students must "consider the needs of their audiences as they compose, edit, and revise."

Another standard emphasizes that "students apply knowledge of language structure, language conventions. . . ." Students need practice with accepted language conventions (e.g., capitalization, punctuation, grammar) in order to develop awareness and consistent application in their writing.

Language Practice is a program designed for students who require additional practice in the basics of effective writing and speaking. Focused practice in key grammar, usage, mechanics, and composition areas helps students gain ownership of essential skills. The logical sequence of the practice exercises, combined with a clear and concise format, allows for easy and independent use.

National Council of Teachers of English and International Reading Association, *Standards for the English Language Arts*, 1996.

Organization

Language Practice provides systematic, focused attention to just one carefully selected skill at a time. Rules are clearly stated at the beginning of each lesson. Key terms are introduced in bold type. The rules are then illustrated with examples and followed by meaningful practice exercises.

Lessons are organized around a series of units. They are arranged in a logical sequence beginning with vocabulary; progressing through sentences, grammar and usage, and mechanics; and culminating with composition skills.

Grades 3 through 8 include a final unit on study skills, which can be assigned as needed. This unit includes such skills as organizing information, following directions, using a dictionary, using the library, and choosing appropriate reference sources.

Skills are reviewed thoroughly in a two-page test at the conclusion of each unit. These unit tests are presented in a standardized test format. The content of each unit is repeated and expanded in subsequent levels as highlighted in the skills correlation chart on pages 6 and 7.

Use

Throughout the program, *Language Practice* stresses the application of language principles. In addition to matching, circling, or underlining elements in a predetermined sentence, lessons ask students to use what they have learned in an original sentence or in rewriting a sentence.

Language Practice is designed for independent use by students who have had instruction in the specific skills covered in these lessons. Copies of the activities can be given to individuals, pairs of students, or small groups for completion. They can also be used as a center activity. If students are familiar with the content, the worksheets can be homework for reviewing and reinforcing skills.

From the beginning, students feel comfortable with the format of the lessons. Each lesson is introduced with a rule at the top of the page and ends with a meaningful exercise at the bottom of the page. Each lesson is clearly labeled, and directions are clear and uncomplicated. Because the format is logical and consistent and the vocabulary is carefully controlled, most students can use *Language Practice* with a high degree of independence. As the teacher, this allows you the time needed to help students on a one-to-one basis.

Special Feature

The process approach to teaching writing provides success for most students. *Language Practice* provides direct support for the teaching of composition and significantly enhances those strategies and techniques commonly associated with the process-writing approach.

Each book includes a composition unit that provides substantial work with important composition skills, such as considering audience, writing topic sentences, selecting supporting details, taking notes, writing reports, and revising and proofreading. Also included in the composition unit is practice with various prewriting activities, such as clustering and brainstorming, which play an important role in process writing. The composition lessons are presented in the same rule-plus-practice format as in other units.

Additional Notes

- Parent Communication. Sign the *Letter to Parents* and send it home with the students. This letter offers suggestions for parental involvement to increase learner success.

- Assessment Test. Use the Assessment Test on pages 8 through 11 to determine the skills your students need to practice.

- Language Terms. Provide each student with a copy of the list of language terms on page 12 to keep for reference throughout the year. Also place a copy in the classroom language arts center for reference.

- Center Activities. Use the worksheets as center activities to give students the opportunity to work cooperatively.

- Have fun. The activities use a variety of strategies to maintain student interest. Watch your students' language improve as skills are applied in structured, relevant practice!

Dear Parent,

During this school year, our class will be working with a language program that covers the basics of effective writing and speaking. To increase your child's language skills, we will be completing activity sheets that provide practice to ensure mastery of these important skills.

From time to time, I may send home activity sheets. To best help your child, please consider the following suggestions:

- Provide a quiet place to work.
- Go over the rules, examples, and directions together.
- Encourage your child to do his or her best.
- Check the lesson when it is complete.
- Go over your child's work, and note improvements as well as concerns.

Help your child maintain a positive attitude about language skills. Let your child know that each lesson provides an opportunity to have fun and to learn. If your child expresses anxiety about these skills, help him or her understand what causes the stress. Then talk about ways to deal with it in a positive way.

Above all, enjoy this time you spend with your child. He or she will feel your support, and skills will improve with each activity completed.

Thank you for your help!

Cordially,

Skills Correlation

Vocabulary	1	2	3	4	5	6	7	8
Sound Words (Onomatopoeia)	■							
Rhyming Words	■	■						
Synonyms	■	■	■	■	■	■	■	■
Antonyms	■	■	■	■	■	■	■	■
Homonyms	■	■	■	■	■	■	■	■
Multiple Meanings/Homographs	■	■	■	■	■	■	■	■
Prefixes and Suffixes			■	■	■	■	■	■
Base and Root Words			■	■	■	■	■	■
Compound Words			■	■	■	■	■	■
Contractions			■	■	■	■	■	■
Idioms						■	■	■
Connotation/Denotation						■	■	■

Sentences	1	2	3	4	5	6	7	8
Word Order in Sentences	■	■						
Recognizing a Sentence	■	■	■	■	■	■	■	■
Subjects and Predicates	■	■	■	■	■	■	■	■
Types of Sentences	■	■	■	■	■	■	■	■
Compound/Complex Sentences			■	■	■	■	■	■
Sentence Combining			■	■	■	■	■	■
Run-On Sentences				■	■	■	■	■
Independent and Subordinate Clauses							■	■
Compound Subjects and Predicates						■	■	■
Direct and Indirect Objects							■	■
Inverted Word Order						■	■	■

Grammar and Usage	1	2	3	4	5	6	7	8
Common and Proper Nouns	■	■	■	■	■	■	■	■
Singular and Plural Nouns	■	■	■	■	■	■	■	■
Possessive Nouns			■	■	■	■	■	■
Appositives						■	■	■
Verbs	■	■	■	■	■	■	■	■
Verb Tense	■	■	■	■	■	■	■	■
Regular/Irregular Verbs	■	■	■	■	■	■	■	■
Subject/Verb Agreement		■	■	■	■	■	■	■
Verb Phrases						■	■	■
Transitive and Intransitive Verbs							■	■
Verbals: Gerunds, Participles, and Infinitives							■	■
Active and Passive Voice							■	■
Mood								■
Pronouns	■	■	■	■	■	■	■	■
Antecedents							■	■
Articles	■	■	■					
Adjectives	■	■	■	■	■	■	■	■
Correct Word Usage (e.g. *may/can, sit/set*)	■	■	■	■	■	■	■	■
Adverbs			■	■	■	■	■	■
Prepositions					■	■	■	■
Prepositional Phrases						■	■	■
Conjunctions						■	■	■
Interjections						■	■	■
Double Negatives								■

Capitalization and Punctuation	1	2	3	4	5	6	7	8
Capitalization: First Word in Sentence	■	■	■	■	■	■	■	
Capitalization: Proper Nouns	■	■	■	■	■	■	■	■
Capitalization: in Letters		■	■	■	■	■	■	■

	1	2	3	4	5	6	7	8
Capitalization and Punctuation (cont'd)								
Capitalization: Abbreviations		■	■	■	■	■	■	■
Capitalization: Titles		■	■	■	■	■	■	■
Capitalization: Proper Adjectives					■	■	■	■
End Punctuation	■	■	■	■	■	■	■	■
Commas		■	■	■	■	■	■	■
Apostrophes in Contractions		■	■	■	■	■	■	■
Apostrophes in Possessives			■	■	■	■	■	■
Quotation Marks			■	■	■	■	■	■
Colons/Semicolons						■	■	■
Hyphens						■	■	■
Composition								
Expanding Sentences					■	■	■	■
Writing a Paragraph		■	■	■	■	■	■	■
Paragraphs: Topic Sentence (main idea)		■	■	■	■	■	■	■
Paragraphs: Supporting Details		■	■	■	■	■	■	■
Order In Paragraphs		■	■	■	■	■	■	
Writing Process:								
Establishing Purpose			■	■		■	■	■
Audience					■	■	■	■
Topic			■	■	■	■	■	■
Outlining				■		■	■	■
Clustering/Brainstorming					■		■	■
Notetaking						■	■	
Revising/Proofreading					■	■	■	■
Types of Writing:								
Letter	■	■	■			■		
"How-to" Paragraph			■					
Invitation			■					
Telephone Message			■					
Conversation				■				
Narrative Paragraph				■				
Comparing and Contrasting					■			
Descriptive Paragraph					■			
Report						■		
Interview							■	
Persuasive Composition								■
Readiness/Study Skills								
Grouping	■							
Letters of Alphabet	■							
Listening	■	■						
Making Comparisons	■	■						
Organizing Information	■	■	■					
Following Directions	■	■	■	■	■			
Alphabetical Order	■	■	■	■	■	■	■	■
Using a Dictionary:								
Definitions		■	■	■	■	■	■	■
Guide Words/Entry Words		■	■	■	■	■	■	■
Syllables			■	■	■	■	■	■
Multiple Meanings						■	■	■
Word Origins						■	■	■
Parts of a Book						■	■	■
Using the Library						■	■	■
Using Encyclopedias					■	■	■	■
Using Reference Books						■	■	■
Using the *Readers' Guide*							■	■
Choosing Appropriate Sources						■	■	■

Skills Correlation
© Steck-Vaughn Publishing Company

Language Practice 2, SV 7158-9

Name _____   Date _____

Assessment Test

A. Look at the picture. Follow the directions.

1. Put an X on the apple.
2. Put an X to the right of the apple.
3. Put an X above the apple.
4. Draw a circle around the apple.

B. Look at the map, and read the directions to Jesse's house. Then answer the questions.

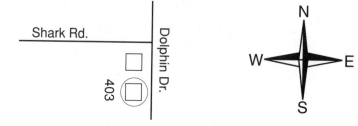

1) Go east on Shark Road.

2) Turn south on Dolphin Drive.

3) Walk down two houses to 403 Dolphin Drive.

1. What direction should you go first? _____

2. What street should you walk on first? _____

3. Which direction should you turn? _____

4. What street should you turn on? _____

5. How many houses down Dolphin Drive is Jesse's house? _____

Name _____   Date _____

C. Cross out the word that does not belong.

1. cup   plate   fork   pen

2. boat   car   name   train

3. tree   door   flower   bush

D. Write the words in alphabetical order.

1. Zena _____

Carol _____

Thomas _____

2. door _____

window _____

carpet _____

E. Underline the words that would be on the same page as the quide words.

day / fish

1. dear   laugh   pig   knob

2. red   sell   egg   dark

3. bait   dust   gold   map

F. Use the dictionary words to answer the questions.

bill	1. a bird's beak 2. a paper that shows how much you owe	**boil**	to heat a liquid until bubbles form
		box	a container used for storing things

1. What word has two meanings? _____

2. What word means "a container used for storing things"? _____

3. What does <u>boil</u> mean? _____

G. Read the words in the box. Then follow the directions.

narrow	pan	angry	short	knew	big

1. Write the words from the box that rhyme.

due_____   man_____

2. Write the words from the box that mean almost the same.

mad _____   large _____

3. Write the words from the box that mean the opposite.

tall _____   wide _____.

H. Circle the correct word to complete each sentence.

1. I went (to, too, two) the park.

2. I am going to (hear, here) the band today.

3. I will meet my friends (there, their).

I. Write T before the telling sentence. Write A before the asking sentence. Write X before the group of words that is not a sentence. Circle the naming parts. Underline the action parts.

_____ **1.** Who took my book?

_____ **2.** To get better.

_____ **3.** I bought some medicine.

J. Circle the special naming words. Underline the action words.

1. Mr. Donaldson grows his own vegetables.

2. He plants some of the vegetables in April.

K. Circle the word that best completes each sentence.

1. Rajib and I (was, were) out of town last week.

2. (We, They) went to Vancouver.

3. Rajib took (a, an) camera.

L. Circle each letter that should be a capital letter. Write the correct punctuation marks for each sentence.

1. mr t r wiggins and i went to daytona beach last saturday sunday and monday

2. rhonda went to the beach last august

3. didnt she take her cat named whiskers

M. Read the paragraph. Circle the main idea, and underline the supporting details.

Julia wanted to bake her friend a cake for his birthday.

First, Julia read the recipe. Then she baked the cake.

After the cake cooled, she put frosting on it.

N. Write 1, 2, 3, or 4 to show what happened first, second, third, and last.

Amy made her bed. First, she pulled up the top sheet. Next, she made the blanket even on all sides. Then she shook the pillow. Last, she laid the quilt across the bed.

_____ Then she shook the pillow.

_____ Next, she made the blanket even on all sides.

_____ Last, she laid the quilt across the bed.

_____ First, she pulled up the top sheet.

Language Terms

abbreviation a short form of a word

action verb a verb that tells an action that the subject is doing

antonym a word that has the opposite meaning of another word

apostrophe a mark used to show where the missing letter or letters would be in a contraction

asking sentence a group of words that asks a question

body the part of a letter that tells what the letter is about

closing the part of a letter that says goodbye

contraction a word formed by joining two other words

dictionary a book of words in ABC order that shows how to spell words and tells what they mean

greeting the part of a letter that tells who will get the letter

heading the part of a letter that tells where and when the letter was written

initial a capital letter with a period after it that stands for a person's name

noun a word that names a person, place, or thing

paragraph a group of sentences about one main idea

plural noun a noun that names more than one person, place, or thing

pronoun a word that takes the place of a noun

proper noun a noun that names a special person, place, or thing and is capitalized

rhyming words words that end with the same sound

sentence a group of words that stands for a complete thought

singular noun a noun that names one person, place, or thing

synonym a word that has the same or almost the same meaning as another word

table of contents a list at the beginning of a book that shows the titles and page numbers of what is in the book

telling sentence a group of words that tells something

verb a word that shows action and tells what a person, place, or thing does

Listening for Directions

- Always pay attention when you are listening for directions.
- Think about what the person is saying.
- Ask for the directions again if you did not hear or understand them.

- **Look at the picture. Follow the directions given by your teacher.**

More Listening for Directions

- Listen carefully to all directions.
- Pay close attention to **key words**, or words that are important.
- Be sure you understand the order in which you are supposed to do things.

  EXAMPLE: You are planting some flowers. First, you prepare the soil. Then you plant the seeds. Finally, you water the seeds.

  Key words numbered in order:

  1) prepare the soil
  2) plant the seeds
  3) water the seeds

- **Listen to the directions. Write the key words in the order in which they should be done.**

1. 1) _____

  2) _____

  3) _____

2. 1) _____

  2) _____

  3) _____

3. 1) _____

  2) _____

  3) _____

4. 1) _____

  2) _____

  3) _____

Following Directions

■ **Read and follow the directions. Write the words that are in the boxes.**

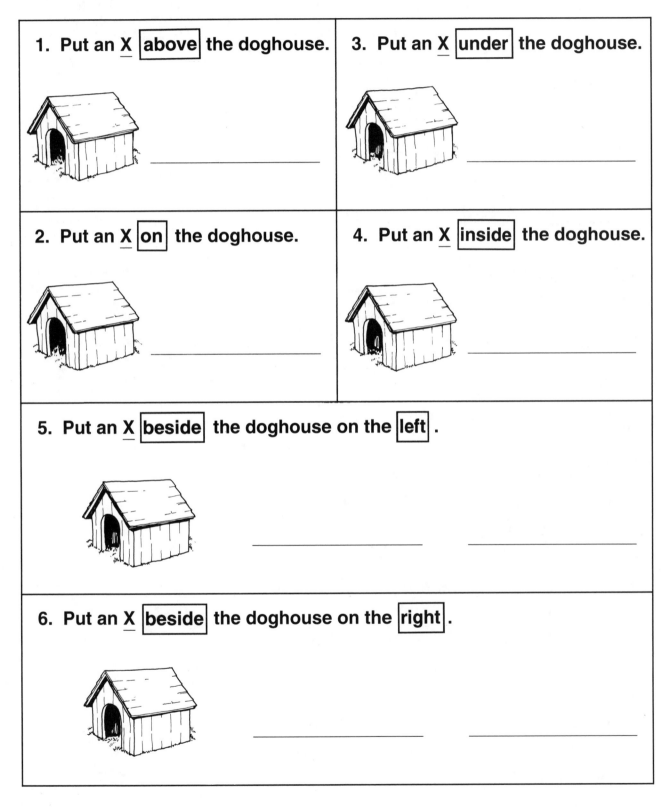

1. Put an $\underline{X}$ above the doghouse.

3. Put an $\underline{X}$ under the doghouse.

2. Put an $\underline{X}$ on the doghouse.

4. Put an $\underline{X}$ inside the doghouse.

5. Put an $\underline{X}$ beside the doghouse on the left .

6. Put an $\underline{X}$ beside the doghouse on the right .

Following Written Directions

■ **Read the sentences. Follow the directions.**

1. A fast horse runs down a wet street. Color
   the horse **brown.** Color the street **gray.**
   Color the water on the street **blue.**

2. A little car has a flat tire. Color the car
   yellow. Color the tires **black.**

3. Two boats go down a river. Color the boats
   pink. Color the sails **blue.**

4. A long flag hangs from a big balloon. Color
   the flag **red.** Color the balloon **purple.**

5. A big tent is beside four tall trees. Color
   the tent **orange.** Color the trees **green.**

6. An airplane flies in the sky. Color
   the airplane **gray.**

Following Directions to a Place

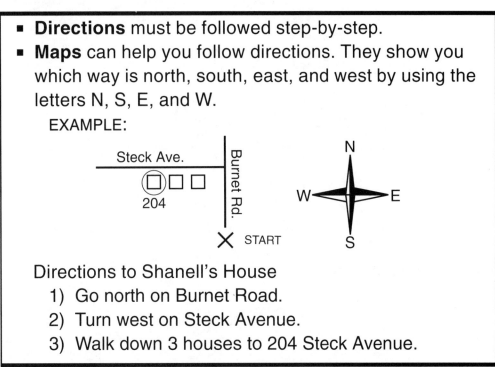

- **Directions** must be followed step-by-step.
- **Maps** can help you follow directions. They show you which way is north, south, east, and west by using the letters N, S, E, and W.

    EXAMPLE:

Directions to Shanell's House
1) Go north on Burnet Road.
2) Turn west on Steck Avenue.
3) Walk down 3 houses to 204 Steck Avenue.

- **Look at the map, and read the directions to Martin's house. Then answer the questions.**

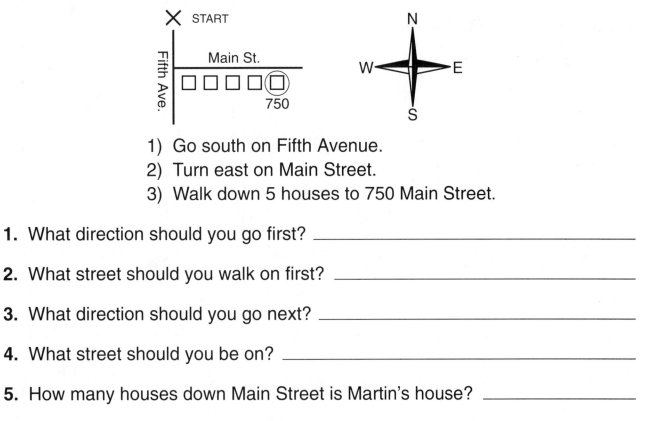

1) Go south on Fifth Avenue.
2) Turn east on Main Street.
3) Walk down 5 houses to 750 Main Street.

1. What direction should you go first? _____

2. What street should you walk on first? _____

3. What direction should you go next? _____

4. What street should you be on? _____

5. How many houses down Main Street is Martin's house? _____

Making Comparisons

■ **Look at the picture of Robert and Sara. Then answer the questions.**

   1. Who has the larger dog? _____

   2. Who has the smaller dog? _____

   3. Who has longer pants? _____

   4. Who has shorter pants? _____

   5. Who has shorter hair? _____

   6. Who has longer hair? _____

   7. Who has lighter hair? _____

   8. Who has darker hair? _____

   9. Who is shorter? _____

   10. Who is taller? _____

Name _____   Date _____

Organizing Information

- **Cross out the word that does not belong.**

1. red   blue   white   ~~turtle~~
2. jump   play   dog   run
3. elephant   Kim   Terry   Susie
4. book   frog   pencil   paper
5. cat   fish   raccoon   sister
6. happy   popcorn   sad   angry
7. breakfast   lunch   candle   supper
8. milk   water   juice   mud
9. cry   doll   ball   game
10. above   under   blue   beside

- **Read the words in the box. Write each word in the correct group.**

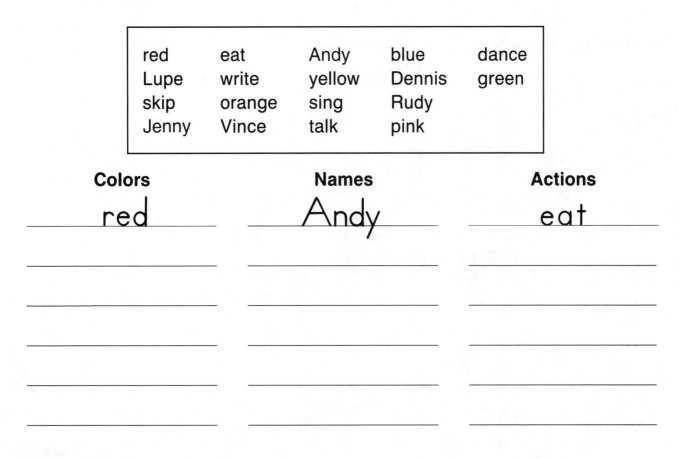

red	eat	Andy	blue	dance
Lupe	write	yellow	Dennis	green
skip	orange	sing	Rudy	
Jenny	Vince	talk	pink	

Colors	Names	Actions
red	Andy	eat

Letters in ABC Order

- **Write the missing letters.**

A B C D _____

_____

_____

_____

- **Write the letter that comes next.**

1. S T U

2. H I ____

3. B C ____

4. P Q ____

5. M N ____

6. K L ____

7. V W ____

8. E F ____

9. X Y ____

10. O P ____

11. D E ____

12. J K ____

- **Write the letter that comes in the middle.**

1. J K L

2. E ____ G

3. Q ____ S

4. F ____ H

5. W ____ Y

6. C ____ E

7. T ____ V

8. M ____ O

9. S ____ U

10. A ____ C

11. L ____ N

12. D ____ F

- **Write the letter that comes before.**

1. A B C

2. ____ T U

3. ____ N O

4. ____ X Y

5. ____ J K

6. ____ F G

7. ____ L M

8. ____ H I

9. ____ Q R

10. ____ S T

11. ____ V W

12. ____ K L

Name _____   Date _____

Words in ABC Order

- **Number the words in ABC order. Then write the words in the right order.**

1.			6.		
_2_ bat	1. _air_		____ neck	1. _____	
_1_ air	2. _bat_		____ owl	2. _____	
_3_ cat	3. _cat_		____ mail	3. _____	

2.			7.		
____ top	1. _____		____ well	1. _____	
____ sea	2. _____		____ us	2. _____	
____ rock	3. _____		____ very	3. _____	

3.			8.		
____ egg	1. _____		____ yes	1. _____	
____ fish	2. _____		____ zoo	2. _____	
____ dog	3. _____		____ X-ray	3. _____	

4.			9.		
____ hat	1. _____		____ pan	1. _____	
____ ice	2. _____		____ oak	2. _____	
____ gate	3. _____		____ nail	3. _____	

5.			10.		
____ joke	1. _____		____ quack	1. _____	
____ lake	2. _____		____ sun	2. _____	
____ king	3. _____		____ rug	3. _____	

Finding Words in a Dictionary

- A **dictionary** is a book of words. The words in a dictionary are in ABC order.
- **Guide words** are at the top of every dictionary page. All the words on the page are in ABC order between these two words.
- The guide word on the left is the first word on the dictionary page.
- The guide word on the right is the last word on the dictionary page.

EXAMPLE: **baby / bed**

baby 〰〰〰〰〰〰   〰〰〰〰〰〰〰〰

〰〰〰〰〰〰〰   **bed** 〰〰〰〰〰〰〰

- **Use the dictionary page in the EXAMPLE to answer these questions.**

1. What is the first word on the above page? _____

2. What is the last word on the above page? _____

- **Choose the pair of guide words below that you would use to find each word.**

fit / fun   race / run   see / sit

1. sent _____ _see/sit_ _____

2. flag _____

3. room _____

4. four _____

5. ranch _____

6. sheep _____

Name _____ Date _____

Using a Dictionary

- A dictionary shows how to spell words.
- A dictionary tells what words mean.

many   a large number

middle   in between

neighbor   someone who lives in the next house

new   never used before

noise   a sound that is loud

open   not shut

paw   the foot of an animal

return   to go back

- **Use the dictionary words to answer the questions.**

1. What word means "in between"? _____

2. What word means "the foot of an animal"? _____

3. What word means "not shut"? _____

4. What word means "a sound that is loud"? _____

5. What word means "a large number"? _____

6. What word means "someone who lives in the next house"?

_____

7. What does <u>return</u> mean? _____

8. What does <u>new</u> mean?

_____

> **always**   at all times
>
> **animal**   a living thing that is not a plant
>
> **bed**   a place to sleep
>
> **dark**   without light
>
> **green**   the color of grass
>
> **hay**   grass cut, and dried, and used as food for cows and horses
>
> **hungry**   needing food
>
> **kitten**   a young cat
>
> **ladder**   a set of steps used to climb up and down
>
> **library**   a building where books are kept

■ **Use the dictionary words to answer the questions.**
Write <u>yes</u> or <u>no</u> on the lines.

1. Is <u>hay</u> something that alligators eat? _____

2. Is the sunrise <u>always</u> in the morning? _____

3. Is a <u>bed</u> a place for swimming? _____

4. Is grass <u>green</u>? _____

5. Is a flower an <u>animal</u>? _____

6. Can you use a <u>ladder</u> to climb to the roof? _____

7. Is it <u>dark</u> outside at night? _____

8. Is a <u>library</u> a place for food? _____

9. Are you <u>hungry</u> after having lunch? _____

10. Is a baby pig called a <u>kitten</u>? _____

More Than One Meaning

> - Some words have more than one meaning.
>   EXAMPLE: **pet**   1. animal kept as a friend
>   2. to stroke
>   Michelle has a **pet** turtle. (meaning 1)
>   Meli loves to **pet** his new puppy. (meaning 2)

- **Read the meanings. Circle the first meaning. Draw a line under the second meaning.**

cold   1. not warm   2. a sickness of

the nose and throat

tie   1. to fasten together with string

2. a cloth worn around the neck

wave   1. moving water   2. to move the

hands back and forth as a greeting

- **Choose the correct word from above to complete each sentence. Write the number of the dictionary meaning that goes with each sentence.**

1. Please _____ tie _____ your shoelaces. |

2. Theo gave Dad a new _____ for his birthday.   ____

3. Leslie splashed in a big _____ at the beach.   ____

4. I always _____ to my friends in school.   ____

5. Put on a coat if you feel _____.   ____

6. Del had a _____ and missed school today.   ____

Table of Contents

> ▪ The **table of contents** is a list at the beginning of a book. It shows the titles and page numbers of what is in the book.

Table of Contents

All Kinds of Pets 5		Fish 24	
Choosing a Pet 7		Birds 26	
Feeding a Pet 9		Rabbits 30	
Exercising a Pet 15		Hamsters 32	
Dogs 17		White Mice 34	
Cats 21			

▪ **Answer these questions.**

1. What is this book about? _____

2. On what page can you read about cats? _____

3. On what page can you read about choosing a pet? _____

4. On what page can you read about exercising a pet? _____

5. What can you read about on page 24? _____

6. What can you read about on page 30? _____

7. How many kinds of pets can you read about? _____

8. On what page can you read about white mice? _____

9. What can you read about on page 17? _____

10. What can you read about on page 26? _____

Name _____   Date _____

Unit 1 Test

Choose the apple with an X on it.

1. A ○   B ○   C ○

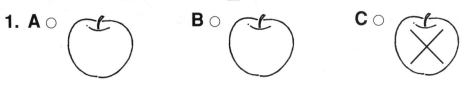

Choose the train with an X beside it, on the right.

2. A ○   B ○   C ○

Choose the butterfly with a circle around it.

3. A ○   B ○   C ○

Look at the map, and read the directions. Then answer the questions.

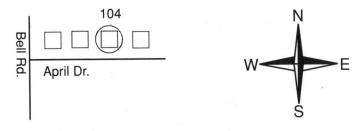

Directions to Roberto's House

  1) Go south on Bell Road.
  2) Turn east on April Drive.
  3) Walk down three houses to 104 April Drive.

4. What direction do you go first?

  A ○ north   **B** ○ east   **C** ○ south

5. How many houses down April Drive is Roberto's house?

  A ○ 4   **B** ○ 3   **C** ○ 2

Choose the word that does not belong.

6. A ○ tree   **B** ○ flower   **C** ○ rug   **10. A** ○ boy   **B** ○ cake   **C** ○ man

7. A ○ milk   **B** ○ name   **C** ○ juice   **11. A** ○ pink   **B** ○ car   **C** ○ boat

8. A ○ cup   **B** ○ plate   **C** ○ pen   **12. A** ○ red   **B** ○ blue   **C** ○ swim

9. A ○ ball   **B** ○ cat   **C** ○ dog   **13. A** ○ car   **B** ○ grass   **C** ○ truck

Choose the list that is in ABC order.

14. A ○ bird   **B** ○ dark   **C** ○ bird   **16. A** ○ nine   **B** ○ rest   **C** ○ mill
          dark   king   king   rest   mill   nine
          king   bird   dark   mill   nine   rest

15. A ○ map   **B** ○ zoo   **C** ○ cat   **17. A** ○ door   **B** ○ fun   **C** ○ door
          zoo   cat   map   knob   door   fun
          cat   map   zoo   fun   knob   knob

Choose the word that would be on the same page as the guide words.

	day / fish			**joke / lost**	
18. A ○ dear	**B** ○ laugh	**C** ○ pig	**21. A** ○ park	**B** ○ key	**C** ○ snow
19. A ○ red	**B** ○ sell	**C** ○ egg	**22. A** ○ today	**B** ○ could	**C** ○ lamp
20. A ○ ball	**B** ○ dog	**C** ○ goat	**23. A** ○ jot	**B** ○ ice	**C** ○ meat

Choose the sentence that goes with definition #1.

24. A ○ I saw a bat at the zoo.

   B ○ Are you afraid of bats?

   C ○ Our team has a new bat.

   D ○ Bats can see at night.

> **bat 1.** a wooden stick used to play baseball
>
> **2.** an animal that flies at night

Name _____   Date _____

Words That Rhyme

> ■ Words that end with the same sound are called **rhyming words**.
>   EXAMPLES: boy—toy   dog—log   cat—sat

■ **Find a rhyming word on the ducks.**
  Write it on the line.

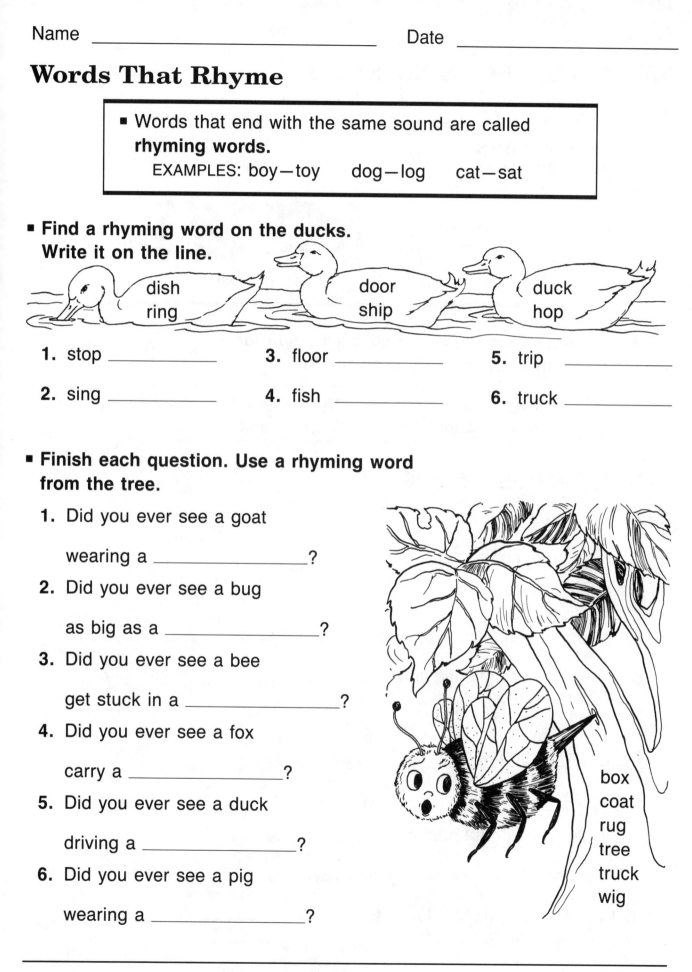

dish
ring

door
ship

duck
hop

1. stop _____   3. floor _____   5. trip _____

2. sing _____   4. fish _____   6. truck _____

■ **Finish each question. Use a rhyming word**
  from the tree.

1. Did you ever see a goat

   wearing a _____?

2. Did you ever see a bug

   as big as a _____?

3. Did you ever see a bee

   get stuck in a _____?

4. Did you ever see a fox

   carry a _____?

5. Did you ever see a duck

   driving a _____?

6. Did you ever see a pig

   wearing a _____?

box
coat
rug
tree
truck
wig

Words That Mean the Same

■ Words that mean almost the same thing are called **synonyms.**
EXAMPLES:

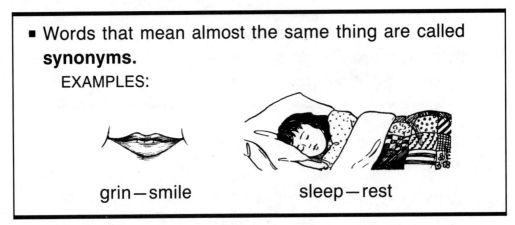

grin — smile   sleep — rest

■ **Read each sentence below. Find a synonym for each underlined word. Write it on the line.**

dog	dad	gift	large	great	home
road	sad	sick	sleep	small	yell

1. I walked across the <u>street</u>. _____

2. I went into my <u>house</u>. _____

3. I was so <u>unhappy</u>. _____

4. I almost felt <u>ill</u>. _____

5. It was my birthday. No one gave me a <u>present</u>. _____

6. Then I saw something <u>little</u>. _____

7. It had <u>big</u> eyes. _____

8. It was a little <u>puppy</u>. _____

9. I began to <u>shout</u>. _____

10. "What a <u>wonderful</u> present!" _____

11. My <u>father</u> did remember my birthday. _____

12. I don't think I will <u>rest</u> tonight. _____

Name _____   Date _____

Words That Mean the Opposite

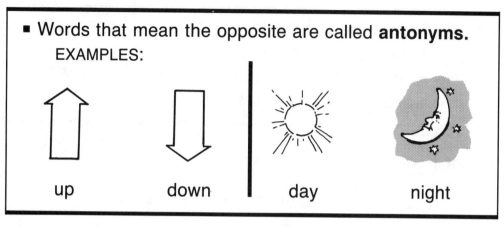

- Words that mean the opposite are called **antonyms.**
  EXAMPLES:

up   down | day   night

■ **Draw a line to the antonym for each underlined word.**

1. a <u>hard</u> bed   dark

2. a <u>short</u> story   happy

3. a <u>light</u> color   long

4. <u>off</u> the table   low

5. a <u>sad</u> movie   on

6. a <u>high</u> bridge   soft

■ **Write the antonym for the underlined word.**

1. When you are not <u>wet</u>, you are _____. (happy, dry)

2. I like to run <u>fast</u>, not _____. (slow, far)

3. When food isn't <u>good</u>, it tastes _____. (hot, bad)

4. Summer is <u>hot</u>, and winter is _____. (cold, snow)

5. A traffic light turns red for <u>stop</u> and green for _____. (high, go)

6. Some questions are <u>easy</u>. Others are _____. (not, hard)

7. My shoes were <u>clean</u>. Then they got _____. (dirty, old)

8. The teacher will answer <u>yes</u> or _____. (maybe, no)

Words That Sound the Same

> - Use <u>hear</u> to mean "to listen to."
>   EXAMPLE: We **hear** the bell ringing.
> - Use <u>here</u> to mean "to this place" or "at this place."
>   EXAMPLE: Bring the ticket **here.**

- **Write <u>hear</u> or <u>here</u>.**

1. Did you _____ that the circus is coming?

2. Is it coming _____ soon?

3. Yes, it will be _____ today.

4. I think I _____ the music now.

5. The parade is almost _____.

6. Come over _____ and watch it with me.

> - Use <u>their</u> to mean "something owned by two or more people."
>   EXAMPLE: The children played with **their** balloons.
> - Use <u>there</u> to mean "in that place."
>   EXAMPLE: The circus tent is over **there.**

- **Write <u>their</u> or <u>there</u>.**

1. The people showed _____ circus tickets.

2. And _____ seats were up high.

3. We put our coats _____ on the seats.

4. Some clowns did _____ tricks for us.

5. Did you see the elephants _____?

More Words That Sound the Same

- Use <u>write</u> to mean "to put words on paper."
  EXAMPLE: Please **write** your name on your paper.
- Use <u>right</u> to mean "correct."
  EXAMPLE: Your answer is **right.**
- Use <u>right</u> to mean "the opposite of left."
  EXAMPLE: Turn **right** to get to my school.

- **Write <u>right</u> or <u>write</u>.**

  1. Chris likes to _____ on the board.

  2. Everything was _____ on Martha's math paper.

  3. We turn _____ to go to the lunchroom.

  4. Our class is learning to _____ stories.

  5. Kim drew the picture on the _____ side.

  6. Did you _____ a letter to your grandma?

  7. Luis can _____ in Spanish.

  8. The teacher marked the _____ answers.

  9. Be sure you do the _____ page.

  10. Jenna will _____ about her birthday party.

  11. James colors with his _____ hand.

- **Write two sentences about school. Use <u>write</u> in one sentence. Use <u>right</u> in the other sentence.**

  1. _____

  2. _____

Other Words That Sound the Same

> - Use <u>two</u> to mean "the number 2."
>   EXAMPLE: **Two** children worked together.
> - Use <u>too</u> to mean "more than enough."
>   EXAMPLE: There are **too** many people on the bus.
> - Use <u>too</u> to mean "also."
>   EXAMPLE: May I help, **too?**
> - Use <u>to</u> to mean "toward" or "to do something."
>   EXAMPLE: Let's go **to** the library **to** find Kim.

- **Write <u>two</u>, <u>too</u>, or <u>to</u>.**

1. The children were working _____ make a class library.

2. Andy had _____ books in his hand.

3. He gave them _____ Ms. Diaz.

4. Ms. Diaz was happy _____ get the books.

5. "We can never have _____ many books," she said.

6. Rosa said she would bring _____ or three books.

7. James wanted to bring some, _____.

8. Joann found a book that was _____ old.

9. Pages started _____ fall out when she picked it up.

10. The bookcase was almost _____ small.

11. Soon everyone would have new books _____ read.

12. We can take out _____ of these books at a time.

13. "Others can enjoy our books, _____," said Chang.

14. Books can be good friends _____ us.

Words That Have Two Meanings

- **Look at each pair of pictures. Read each sentence. Then write the letter of the correct meaning on the line.**

bat

a.   b.

1. _____ Tony has a wooden bat.

2. _____ The bat sleeps during the day.

3. _____ The bat broke when Alberto hit the ball.

pitcher

a.   b.

7. _____ The pitcher threw the ball too low.

8. _____ I put some juice in the pitcher.

9. _____ The pitcher of milk was empty.

plant

a.   b.

4. _____ Kendra wants to plant a tree.

5. _____ The farmer will plant his crops in the fall.

6. _____ Jody grew a plant at school.

light

a.   b.

10. _____ I will turn on the light.

11. _____ The puppy is light.

12. _____ There is only one light in my room.

Name _____   Date _____

Unit 2 Test

Choose the correct word to complete each sentence.

1. A word that rhymes with <u>bake</u> is ___.

   A ○ take   **B** ○ goat   **C** ○ cook

2. A word that rhymes with <u>ship</u> is ___.

   A ○ boat   **B** ○ drip   **C** ○ shut

3. <u>Grin</u> means almost the same as ___.

   A ○ pin   **B** ○ cry   **C** ○ smile

4. <u>House</u> means almost the same as ___.

   A ○ trip   **B** ○ home   **C** ○ mouse

5. The opposite of <u>long</u> is ___.

   A ○ song   **B** ○ tall   **C** ○ short

6. The opposite of <u>hot</u> is ___.

   A ○ cold   **B** ○ warm   **C** ○ pot

7. Did you ___ about the prize?

   A ○ hear   **B** ○ here   **C** ○ there

8. Jenna and Chris will bring ___ books to the library.

   A ○ there   **B** ○ their   **C** ○ hear

9. I have learned how to ___ all the spelling words.

   A ○ right   **B** ○ wrote   **C** ○ write

10. Our class wants ___ play outside today.

    A ○ to   **B** ○ too   **C** ○ two

11. I have ___ many books to carry!

    A ○ to   **B** ○ too   **C** ○ two

Name _____   Date _____

Look at each pair of pictures. Read each sentence. Then choose the letter of the correct meaning for the underlined word.

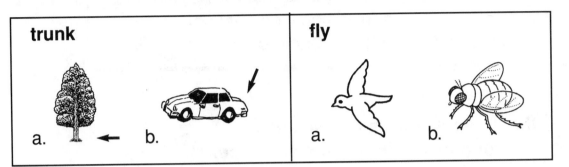

trunk   a.   b.   **fly**   a.   b.

12. Joanne got the packages out of the <u>trunk</u>.

    A ○ meaning <u>a</u>   **B** ○ meaning <u>b</u>

13. I sat beside the tree and leaned against its <u>trunk</u>.

    A ○ meaning <u>a</u>   **B** ○ meaning <u>b</u>

14. There was a large hole in the <u>trunk</u> of the tree.

    A ○ meaning <u>a</u>   **B** ○ meaning <u>b</u>

15. The spare tire for the car is in the <u>trunk</u>.

    A ○ meaning <u>a</u>   **B** ○ meaning <u>b</u>

16. There is a <u>fly</u> on the wall.

    A ○ meaning <u>a</u>   **B** ○ meaning <u>b</u>

17. Geese usually <u>fly</u> south for the winter.

    A ○ meaning <u>a</u>   **B** ○ meaning <u>b</u>

18. An ostrich is a bird that cannot <u>fly</u>.

    A ○ meaning <u>a</u>   **B** ○ meaning <u>b</u>

19. The <u>fly</u> kept buzzing in my ear.

    A ○ meaning <u>a</u>   **B** ○ meaning <u>b</u>

20. I saw the bird <u>fly</u> to its nest.

    A ○ meaning <u>a</u>   **B** ○ meaning <u>b</u>

Sentences

> ■ A **sentence** is a group of words that tells or asks something. It stands for a complete thought.
> EXAMPLES: Friends play. Cars go fast.

■ **Write yes if the group of words is a sentence.**
Write no if the group of words is not a sentence.

1. ___no___ A long time ago.

2. _____ The class went to the park.

3. _____ Near the tree.

4. _____ Ten children played.

5. _____ Mark hit the ball.

6. _____ A dog chased the ball.

7. _____ Bill and Tom.

8. _____ Ran and played all day.

9. _____ Everyone had fun.

10. _____ Jan lost a new red shoe.

11. _____ We ate lunch.

12. _____ Too hot for us.

13. _____ The boys and girls talked.

14. _____ Some people.

15. _____ Sang songs.

16. _____ Then we went home.

More Sentences

- **Draw lines between the groups of words to make sentences. Then read the sentences.**

1. Mrs. Brown   live in our building.
2. Our building   is made of wood.
3. Four families   lives on my street.

4. Our school   was climbing the tree.
5. Jennifer   went on a picnic.
6. The sun   shone all day.

7. Corn and beans   fed the baby goat.
8. The wagon   has a broken wheel.
9. The mother goat   grow on a farm.

10. The boat   sailed in strong winds.
11. The fisher   were sold in the store.
12. Some of the fish   caught seven fish.

13. Our team   hit the ball a lot.
14. Our batters   won ten games.
15. The ballpark   was full of fans.

- **Write a sentence about your birthday.**

_____

_____

- **Write a sentence about your house or apartment.**

_____

_____

Name _____   Date _____

Word Order in Sentences

> ■ Words in a sentence must be in an order that makes sense.
>   EXAMPLES: Grandpa plays baseball.
>   My sister writes stories.

■ **Write these words in an order that makes sense.**

1. brother My apples eats

   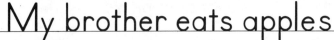 My brother eats apples _____.

2. drinks Elizabeth milk

   _____.

3. butter peanut Kim likes

   _____.

4. Justin bread wants

   _____.

5. corn plants Chris

   _____.

6. a fish Chang caught

   _____.

7. breakfast cooks Dad

   _____.

8. his shares Shawn lunch

   _____.

9. the Rosa grew carrot

   _____.

10. the looks at Kate pie

   _____.

Name _____ Date _____

Telling Sentences

- A **telling sentence** is a group of words that tells something.
  EXAMPLES: I fed my pony.
  Ponies like to run and play.

- **Write telling on the line before the group of words if it is a telling sentence. Leave the line blank if it is not a sentence.**

_____telling_____   **1.** Josh loves his pony.

_____   **2.** His name is Zip.

_____   **3.** Fast horses.

_____   **4.** Zip can run fast.

_____   **5.** He eats apples.

_____   **6.** Over the hill.

_____   **7.** Zip runs to Josh.

_____   **8.** Zip has a long tail.

_____   **9.** Josh and his mother.

_____   **10.** His hair is soft.

_____   **11.** After school.

_____   **12.** Josh likes to play with Zip.

_____   **13.** In the barn.

_____   **14.** Josh brushes Zip.

_____   **15.** You can ride Zip, too.

Asking Sentences

> ■ An **asking sentence** is a group of words that asks a question. You can answer an asking sentence.
> EXAMPLES: How old are you? Where do you live?

■ **Write asking on the line before the group of words if it is an asking sentence. Leave the line blank if the group of words is not a sentence.**

asking	**1.** Is this your friend?
_____	**2.** Where does she live?
_____	**3.** She in town?
_____	**4.** How was school today?
_____	**5.** Music and art?
_____	**6.** Do you want a snack?
_____	**7.** Where are the apples?
_____	**8.** Look in the?
_____	**9.** When does school begin?
_____	**10.** Do you have any brothers?
_____	**11.** Where can we work?
_____	**12.** The kitchen in?
_____	**13.** Can you ride a bike?
_____	**14.** Yes, I?
_____	**15.** Why did Sarah cry?

Kinds of Sentences

- **Write telling for telling sentences.**
  Write asking for asking sentences.

_____ 1. Where is the toy store?

_____ 2. The toy store is near school.

_____ 3. Do you like kites?

_____ 4. There are balloons and balls.

_____ 5. Some toys can play music.

_____ 6. Who plays with markers?

_____ 7. I have a few games.

_____ 8. Mom will buy a puzzle.

_____ 9. Where are the bikes?

_____ 10. When will you play with bubbles?

- **Read the sentences. Write each sentence under
  the correct heading.**

I went to the toy store.   Are there any puzzles?
Which toy do you want?   I picked a game.

Telling Sentences

_____

_____

Asking Sentences

_____

_____

Name _____   Date _____

Naming Part of Sentences

> - The naming part of a sentence tells who or what the sentence is about.
>   EXAMPLES: **Three mice** run away. **The cat** plays with a ball.

- **Circle the naming part of each sentence.**

1. (My family and I) live on a busy street.

2. Sally Harper found a bird.

3. Miss Jenkins drives very slowly.

4. Mr. Olson walks his dog.

5. Henry throws to his dog.

6. Mr. Byrne cuts his grass.

7. Mrs. Lee picks up her children.

8. Mr. and Mrs. Diaz shop for food.

9. Jeanine plays in the park.

10. Mr. Wolf brings the mail.

11. Sammy Taft brings the paper.

12. Mr. O'Dowd cooks dinner.

13. Nina paints the house.

14. Some children plant a garden.

15. Mrs. Clark washes her windows.

16. Carolyn and Albert plant flower seeds.

17. Julie waters the garden.

Action Part of Sentences

> ■ The action part of a sentence tells what someone or something does.
>   EXAMPLES: Three mice **run away**. The cat **plays with a ball.**

■ **Circle the action part of each sentence.**

1. My family and I live on a busy street.

2. Sally Harper found a bird.

3. Miss Jenkins drives very slowly.

4. Mr. Olson walks his dog.

5. Henry throws to his dog.

6. Mr. Byrne cuts his grass.

7. Mrs. Lee picks up her children.

8. Mr. and Mrs. Diaz shop for food.

9. Jeanine plays in the park.

10. Mr. Wolf brings the mail.

11. Sammy Taft brings the paper.

12. Mr. O'Dowd cooks dinner.

13. Nina paints the house.

14. Some children plant a garden.

15. Mrs. Clark washes her windows.

16. Carolyn and Albert plant flower seeds.

17. Julie waters the garden.

Sentence Parts

- **Choose a naming part to complete each sentence.**

Lions	Birds	A pig	A cat	My dog	Zebras	Fish

1. _____Lions_____ roar loudly in their cages.

2. _____ have black and white stripes.

3. _____ rolls in the mud.

4. _____ plays with a ball of yarn.

5. _____ chews his new bone.

6. _____ swim in water.

7. _____ fly in the sky.

- **Choose an action part to complete each sentence.**

barks	buzz	fly	hops	moo	quack	roar

1. Robins and blackbirds _____fly_____.

2. Yellow bees _____.

3. My little dog _____.

4. Mother Duck and her babies _____.

5. A rabbit with big feet _____.

6. Angry lions _____.

7. All the cows on the farm _____.

- **Write a sentence about an animal that you like.
  Circle the naming part. Underline the action part.**

_____

Unit 3 Test

Choose whether the group of words is a sentence.

1. Seven children from my class.   **A** ○ yes   **B** ○ no

2. Joe and Margaret are best friends.   **A** ○ yes   **B** ○ no

3. Got here today.   **A** ○ yes   **B** ○ no

4. I can swim.   **A** ○ yes   **B** ○ no

5. Kathy doesn't know if.   **A** ○ yes   **B** ○ no

6. The girls and boys.   **A** ○ yes   **B** ○ no

7. We will walk today.   **A** ○ yes   **B** ○ no

8. Gina studied for the test.   **A** ○ yes   **B** ○ no

9. My father needs.   **A** ○ yes   **B** ○ no

10. Uncle Jeremy is out of town.   **A** ○ yes   **B** ○ no

Choose the sentences that are in an order that makes sense.

11. **A** ○ It time what is?
    B ○ What time is it?
    C ○ Time what it is?

12. **A** ○ Is caught my kite in a tree.
    B ○ My kite is caught in a tree.
    C ○ Tree is a my kite caught is.

13. **A** ○ Tomorrow my birthday is.
    B ○ My is tomorrow birthday.
    C ○ My birthday is tomorrow.

14. **A** ○ Circus the is fun.
    B ○ The circus is fun.
    C ○ Fun the circus is.

15. **A** ○ My sister went to the store.
    B ○ My store went to the sister.
    C ○ To the store my went sister.

16. **A** ○ Tina likes to ride horses.
    B ○ Ride horses Tina likes to.
    C ○ Likes to ride horses Tina.

17. **A** ○ Rang the telephone.
    B ○ The telephone rang.
    C ○ The rang telephone.

18. **A** ○ His Toby plays with puppy.
    B ○ Puppy plays Toby with his.
    C ○ Toby plays with his puppy.

Choose <u>telling</u> or <u>asking</u> for each sentence.

19. Daisy is my dog.   **A** ○ telling   **B** ○ asking

20. She can follow directions.   **A** ○ telling   **B** ○ asking

21. Does she have a doghouse?   **A** ○ telling   **B** ○ asking

22. She stays in our house.   **A** ○ telling   **B** ○ asking

23. Where does Daisy play?   **A** ○ telling   **B** ○ asking

24. She plays in the yard.   **A** ○ telling   **B** ○ asking

25. What is Daisy doing?   **A** ○ telling   **B** ○ asking

26. Daisy likes to dig in the yard.   **A** ○ telling   **B** ○ asking

27. Daisy hid her bone.   **A** ○ telling   **B** ○ asking

28. Do you know where her bone is?   **A** ○ telling   **B** ○ asking

**Choose <u>naming part</u> or <u>action part</u> to tell about
the underlined words in each sentence.**

29. Megan <u>studied for her test</u>.   **A** ○ naming part   **B** ○ action part

30. <u>The children on my street</u> play together.   **A** ○ naming part   **B** ○ action part

31. My little sister <u>loves to play soccer</u>.   **A** ○ naming part   **B** ○ action part

32. I <u>will go to school</u>.   **A** ○ naming part   **B** ○ action part

33. <u>My brother</u> loves to swim.   **A** ○ naming part   **B** ○ action part

34. Janet's grandparents <u>went to the coast</u>.   **A** ○ naming part   **B** ○ action part

35. The winner <u>gets a blue ribbon</u>.   **A** ○ naming part   **B** ○ action part

36. <u>A farmer</u> plants crops.   **A** ○ naming part   **B** ○ action part

Naming Words

> - A **noun** is a word that names a person, place, or thing. The words a, an, and the are clues that show a noun is near.
>   EXAMPLES: a **man,** the **yard,** an **elephant**

- **Find the nouns, or naming words, below.
  Write the nouns on the lines.**

apple	car	eat	hear	rug
bird	chair	girl	hot	tree
boy	desk	gone	over	truck
came	dirty	grass	pen	up

1. _apple_   5. _____   9. _____

2. _____   6. _____   10. _____

3. _____   7. _____   11. _____

4. _____   8. _____   12. _____

- **Draw lines under the two nouns in each sentence.
  Write the nouns on the lines.**

1. The girl eats an apple.   _____ _____

2. A bird flies to the tree.   _____ _____

3. A chair is by the desk.   _____ _____

4. A boy sits in the chair.   _____ _____

5. The girl plays with a truck. _____ _____

6. The truck is on the rug.   _____ _____

Special Naming Words

> ■ A noun is a word that names a person, place, or thing. A **proper noun** is a word that names a special person, place, or thing. A proper noun begins with a capital letter.
>
> EXAMPLES: **Noun**   **Proper Noun**
> girl   Karen Stone
> park   City Park
> bread   Tasty Bread

■ **Find the proper nouns below. Write the proper nouns on the lines.**

baseball	China	man	prince
Bob's Bikes	Elf Corn	New York City	robin
Bridge Road	Gabriel	Ohio	State Street
children	Linda	Pat Green	village

1. _Bob's Bikes_   6. _____

2. _____   7. _____

3. _____   8. _____

4. _____   9. _____

5. _____   10. _____

■ **Draw a line under the proper noun in each sentence. Write each proper noun on the line.**

1. I bought apples at Hill's Store. _____

2. The store is on Baker Street. _____

3. It is near Stone Library. _____

4. I gave an apple to Emily Fuller. _____

Name _____   Date _____

One and More Than One

> ■ Add -s to most nouns to make them name more than one.   EXAMPLE: a book, four books

■ **Rewrite these nouns to make them name more than one.**

1. cap _____

2. chair _____

3. girl _____

4. tree _____

5. flag _____

6. boy _____

> ■ Add -es to nouns that end with -x, -ss, -ch, or -sh to make them name more than one.
> EXAMPLES: fox, ten fox**es**   class, a few class**es**
> branch, five branch**es**   bush, six bush**es**

■ **Rewrite these nouns to make them name more than one.**

1. lunch _____

2. dress _____

3. glass _____

4. dish _____

5. box _____

6. watch _____

■ **Write the word on the line that will complete each phrase. Add -s or -es.**

1. two _____
              (pond)

2. many _____
                (pig)

3. three _____
                (brush)

4. ten _____
              (frog)

5. six _____
              (wish)

6. five _____
              (bench)

7. four _____
              (ax)

8. a few _____
                (ball)

Action Words

> - A **verb** is a word that shows action. Verbs tell what a person, place, or thing does.
>   EXAMPLES: dogs **play**   I **eat**   Pat **reads**

- **Draw a line from each noun to the correct verb, or action word.**

Nouns	Verbs
1. The boy	hops.
2. The baby	sing.
3. The rabbit	bark.
4. The birds	cries.
5. The dogs	reads.

- **Draw a line under the verb in each sentence.**

    1. Eric runs by Mr. and Mrs. Wilson's house.

    2. He kicks a football into the air.

    3. The ball breaks the Wilsons' window.

    4. Mrs. Wilson looks out the door.

    5. Mr. Wilson shakes his head.

    6. Eric's face turns red.

    7. Eric runs inside his house.

    8. Mother talks to Eric about the window.

    9. Mother sends Eric to the Wilsons' house.

    10. Eric talks to the Wilsons.

    11. Eric pays for the window.

    12. Eric shakes hands with the Wilsons.

    13. Eric only plays football at the park now.

Naming Word or Action Word

- **Draw a line under the two nouns, or naming words, in each sentence.**

    1. Our <u>class</u> is in our <u>room</u>.

    2. Our teacher reads us stories.

    3. Some stories are about elephants.

    4. Elephants are very big animals.

- **Draw a line under the verb, or action word, in each sentence.**

    1. An elephant <u>takes</u> a bath.

    2. Zoo workers put water on the elephant.

    3. They rub soap all over the elephant.

    4. Workers wash behind the elephant's ears.

    5. Workers pour more water on the elephant.

- **Read the sentences. Write <u>noun</u> or <u>verb</u> for each underlined word.**

    1. The wind <u>blows</u> hard today. _____

    2. <u>Eddie</u> and Susan fly their kites. _____

    3. The <u>kites</u> go up high. _____

    4. They <u>climb</u> into the sky. _____

    5. Eddie's kite <u>string</u> breaks. _____

    6. His kite <u>flies</u> away. _____

    7. <u>Susan</u> shares her kite with Eddie. _____

    8. Eddie <u>smiles</u>. _____

    9. He hugs his best <u>friend</u>. _____

Adding *-ed* or *-ing* to Verbs

- To show that something happened in the past, add -ed to most verbs.
    EXAMPLE: Don **visited** Liz yesterday.
- To show that something is happening now, you can add -ing to most verbs.
    EXAMPLE: Sue is **visiting** Liz now.

- **Draw a line under the correct verb.**

    1. Terry and Joe (played, playing) basketball last week.

    2. Jenny (called, calling) to them.

    3. She (wanted, wanting) to play, too.

    4. The boys (laughed, laughing) at her.

    5. But Jenny (jumped, jumping) for the ball.

    6. She (played, playing) well.

    7. Terry and Joe are not (laughed, laughing) anymore.

    8. Now Jenny is (played, playing) on their team.

    9. Their friends are (watched, watching) them play.

    10. Everyone is (talked, talking) about all the games they've won.

- **Add -ed or -ing to each verb. Then rewrite each sentence.**

    1. Carmen is finish _____ her work now. _____

    _____

    2. Carmen help _____ Grandma cook yesterday. _____

    _____

    3. Grandma is cook_____ some soup today. _____

    _____

Name _____   Date _____

Using *Is* or *Are*

> - Use <u>is</u> and <u>are</u> to tell about something that is happening now.
> - Use <u>is</u> to tell about one person, place, or thing.
>   EXAMPLE: Judy **is** going.
> - Use <u>are</u> to tell about more than one person, place, or thing.
>   EXAMPLES: Lynne and Ed **are** skating.
>   The cats **are** sleeping.
> - Use <u>are</u> with the word <u>you</u>.
>   EXAMPLES: You **are** lost. **Are** you happy?

- **Write <u>is</u> or <u>are</u>.**

1. We ___are___ going to the park.

2. Al _____ going, too.

3. Kate and Calvin _____ running.

4. She _____ the faster runner.

5. Where _____ the twins?

6. They _____ climbing a tree.

7. You _____ going to climb, too.

8. Bill _____ looking at the ducks.

9. The children_____ having fun.

One duck
is here.

Many ducks
are here.

- **Write one sentence about a park using <u>is</u>.**
  Write one sentence about a park using <u>are</u>.

1. (is) _____

2. (are) _____

Using *Was* or *Were*

- Use <u>was</u> and <u>were</u> to tell about something that happened in the past.
- Use <u>was</u> to tell about one person, place, or thing.
    EXAMPLE: My bat **was** on the step.
- Use <u>were</u> to tell about more than one person, place, or thing.
    EXAMPLES: Ten people **were** there.
    The books **were** lost.
- Use <u>were</u> with the word <u>you</u>.
    EXAMPLES: You **were** late. **Were** you home?

- **Write <u>was</u> or <u>were</u>.**

1. The children _____ indoors while it rained.

2. José _____ reading a book.

3. Scott and Jay _____ playing checkers.

4. Ann, Roy, and Jamie _____ playing cards.

5. Sara and Bill _____ talking.

6. Nicky _____ beating a drum.

7. I _____ drawing pictures.

8. You _____ dancing.

9. Steve _____ tired of staying inside.

- **Write one sentence about a rainy day using <u>was</u>. Write one sentence about a rainy day using <u>were</u>.**

1. (was) _____

2. (were) _____

Name _____   Date _____

Using *See, Sees,* or *Saw*

> - Use <u>see</u> or <u>sees</u> to tell what is happening now.
>   EXAMPLES: One boy **sees** a dog.
>   Two boys **see** a dog.
> - Use <u>see</u> with the words <u>you</u> and <u>I</u>.
>   EXAMPLES: I **see** a dog. Do you **see** a dog?
> - Use <u>saw</u> to tell what happened in the past.
>   EXAMPLE: Justin **saw** Natalie last week.

- **Write <u>see</u>, <u>sees</u>, or <u>saw</u>.**

1. Today Mike _____ sees _____ his friend Lori.

2. He _____ her last Monday.

3. Lori _____ Mike paint now.

4. My dad _____ Mike paint now, too.

5. Mike _____ a beautiful sky last night.

6. He _____ pink in the sky on Sunday.

7. Grandpa and I _____ some trains now.

8. We _____ many trains on my last birthday.

9. We _____ old and new trains last winter.

10. Today I can _____ the train show.

- **Write <u>see</u>, <u>sees</u>, or <u>saw</u>. Rewrite each sentence.**

1. Last week we _____ Lee. _____

_____

2. Lee _____ my painting now. _____

_____

Using *Run, Runs,* or *Ran*

> ■ Use run or runs to tell what is happening now.
>   EXAMPLES: One horse **runs.** Two horses **run.**
> ■ Use run with the words you and I.
>   EXAMPLES: I **run** in the park. Do you **run?**
> ■ Use ran to tell what happened in the past.
>   EXAMPLE: Yesterday we **ran** to the park.

■ **Write run, runs, or ran. Rewrite each sentence.**

1. Horses _____ wild long ago. _____

_____

2. A horse can _____ ten miles every day. _____

_____

3. Can you _____ as fast as a horse? _____

_____

4. Mandy _____ in a race last week. _____

_____

5. Andy _____ home from school now. _____

_____

6. Now Mandy _____ after Andy. _____

_____

7. How far can you _____? _____

_____

Using *Give*, *Gives*, or *Gave*

- Use <u>give</u> or <u>gives</u> to tell what is happening now.
  EXAMPLES: One student **gives** a gift.
  Two students **give** a gift.
- Use <u>give</u> with the words <u>you</u> and I.
  EXAMPLES: I **give** a gift. Do you **give** one?
- Use <u>gave</u> to tell what happened in the past.
  EXAMPLE: Jeff **gave** me a present yesterday.

- **Write <u>give</u>, <u>gives</u>, or <u>gave</u>.**

  1. Can you _____ the animals some food?

  2. Sandi _____ them water yesterday.

  3. Juan _____ the chickens corn now.

  4. Chickens _____ us eggs to eat yesterday.

  5. We _____ the kittens some milk last night.

  6. Who _____ hay to the cow then?

  7. Our cow _____ us milk yesterday.

  8. I _____ food to the pigs last Monday.

  9. Mary _____ food to the sheep now.

  10. Sheep _____ us wool for warm coats.

- **Write three sentences about gifts using <u>give</u>,
  <u>gives</u>, and <u>gave</u>.**

  1. _____

  2. _____

  3. _____

Using *Do* or *Does*

> - Use <u>does</u> to tell about one person, place, or thing.
>   EXAMPLE: William **does** the work.
> - Use <u>do</u> to tell about more than one person, place, or thing.   EXAMPLE: They **do** the work.
> - Also use <u>do</u> with the words <u>you</u> and I.
>   EXAMPLES: I **do** the work. You **do** the work.

- **Write <u>do</u> or <u>does</u>.**

   1. We _____ a lot of work in the house.

   2. My dad _____ all the dishes.

   3. My mom _____ the windows.

   4. My sister _____ the sweeping.

   5. My grandma _____ the sewing.

   6. I _____ the floor.

   7. My little brother _____ the dusting.

   8. I _____ not cook the dinner.

   9. My little sister _____ put away toys.

   10. We all _____ some work in our house.

   11. It is fun to _____ it together.

   12. We _____ other things together, too.

- **Write one sentence about yourself using <u>do</u>.**
  Write one sentence about a friend using <u>does</u>.

   1. _____

   2. _____

Name _____   Date _____

Using *Has, Have,* or *Had*

- Use <u>has</u> to tell about one person, place, or thing.
    EXAMPLE: Jesse **has** a bird.
- Use <u>have</u> to tell about more than one person, place, or thing.
    EXAMPLE: Cars **have** tires.
- Use <u>have</u> with the words <u>you</u> and <u>I</u>.
    EXAMPLES: You **have** new shoes. I **have** fun.
- Use <u>had</u> to tell about the past.
    EXAMPLES: My dogs **had** fleas.
    Bill **had** a cat last year.

- **Write <u>has</u>, <u>have</u>, or <u>had</u>.**

1. My brother _____ a pet fish last year.

2. Now Dan _____ a pet mouse.

3. The pets _____ good homes now.

4. I _____ a football now.

5. Now Dana _____ a pair of roller skates, too.

6. Yesterday Dawn _____ a full balloon.

7. Now the balloon _____ a hole in it.

8. She _____ the money to buy another balloon today.

9. You _____ many friends now.

10. Your friends _____ fun together last Saturday.

11. Last week I _____ supper with Eric.

12. Now he _____ supper with me.

13. Last night Jim _____ many things to do.

14. Mother said he _____ to fix his bike last night.

Pronouns

> ■ A **pronoun** is a word that takes the place of a noun. Some pronouns are <u>he</u>, <u>she</u>, <u>it</u>, <u>we</u>, <u>you</u>, <u>they</u>, and <u>I</u>.
>
> EXAMPLE: <u>Bill</u> plays with James. <u>He</u> plays with James.

■ **Rewrite these sentences. Choose a pronoun to take the place of the words that are underlined.**

He	She	It	We	They

1. <u>Alicia</u> got a gift.

She got a gift.

2. <u>The gift</u> was for her birthday.

_____

3. <u>James</u> brought the gift.

_____

4. <u>Kim and Tim</u> found a box.

_____

5. <u>Ellen and I</u> are going to the party.

_____

6. <u>Rosa and Luis</u> will wear hats.

_____

7. <u>Sue</u> likes punch.

_____

8. <u>The party</u> will end soon.

_____

Using *I* or *Me*

> - Use I in the naming part of the sentence.
>   EXAMPLES: **I** went to the movie.
>   Dad and **I** played cards.
> - Use me after a verb, or action word.
>   EXAMPLES: Mom gave **me** the ball.
>   Mrs. Ford asked Kathy and **me.**

- **Circle I or me.**

1. (I, Me) wanted a job.

2. Molly and (I, me) tried to make money.

3. Mr. Garcia gave Molly and (I, me) a job.

4. Mr. Garcia told (I, me) to cut his grass.

5. Molly and (I, me) made four dollars each.

6. (I, Me) will buy a treat for us.

- **Write I or me.**

1. _____ went on a trip.

2. Dad gave _____ a new fishing pole.

3. Ben and _____ went to the lake.

4. _____ had a good time fishing.

5. Mom and _____ went on a hike.

6. My sister read Ben and _____ a story.

7. Uncle Warren and _____ sang songs.

8. _____ was tired when we got home.

Using *A* or *An*

- Use <u>an</u> before words that begin with a vowel sound.
  EXAMPLES: **an** apple, **an** egg
- The vowels are <u>a</u>, <u>e</u>, <u>i</u>, <u>o</u>, and <u>u</u>.
- Use <u>a</u> before words that begin with a consonant sound.
  EXAMPLES: **a** car, **a** skate

a car   an apple

a rope   an egg

a skate   an iron

- **Write <u>a</u> or <u>an</u>.**

1. _____ arm

2. _____ dog

3. _____ hat

4. _____ ant

5. _____ cat

6. _____ elf

7. _____ ear

8. _____ office

9. _____ fire

10. _____ cow

11. _____ can

12. _____ tree

13. _____ inch

14. _____ ax

15. _____ top

16. _____ boat

17. _____ duck

18. _____ oven

19. _____ eagle

20. _____ pet

21. _____ uncle

22. Randy put _____ apple in my box.

23. Victor has _____ old go-cart.

24. Linda has two balls and _____ bat.

Using Words That Compare

- Add -er to most words to compare two people or
  two things.   EXAMPLE: Matt is **fast.**
  Clare is **faster** than Matt.
- Add -est to most words to compare more than two
  people or two things.   EXAMPLE: Leo is the
  fastest of the three children.

- **Add -er or -est. Write the sentences.**

1. Dad is young_____ than Mom.

_____

2. Kim is the old_____ of four children.

_____

3. An ant is small_____ than a pig.

_____

4. That snake is the long_____ of the six at the zoo.

_____

5. The barn is tall_____ than the house.

_____

6. Alex is strong_____ than Michael.

_____

7. That blue chair is the soft_____ in the room.

_____

Unit 4 Test

Choose <u>noun</u> or <u>verb</u> for each underlined word.

1. The swimming <u>pool</u> opens today.   **A** ○ noun   **B** ○ verb

2. I <u>jump</u> in the deep water.   **A** ○ noun   **B** ○ verb

3. <u>Kenny</u> and I race across the pool.   **A** ○ noun   **B** ○ verb

4. The <u>water</u> feels cool.   **A** ○ noun   **B** ○ verb

5. Some of my <u>friends</u> are at the pool.   **A** ○ noun   **B** ○ verb

6. The pool <u>closes</u> soon.   **A** ○ noun   **B** ○ verb

Choose whether the underlined words are proper nouns.

7. Is <u>Lisa</u> going to the party?   **A** ○ yes   **B** ○ no

8. Our whole <u>team</u> is going to the party.   **A** ○ yes   **B** ○ no

9. The party will be at <u>Pizza Parade</u>.   **A** ○ yes   **B** ○ no

10. Pizza Parade is on <u>Coral Drive</u>.   **A** ○ yes   **B** ○ no

11. What <u>day</u> of the week is the party?   **A** ○ yes   **B** ○ no

12. The party is on <u>Saturday</u>.   **A** ○ yes   **B** ○ no

Choose the noun that means more than one.

13. **A** ○ bag   **B** ○ yard   **C** ○ boxes

14. **A** ○ bands   **B** ○ engine   **C** ○ dog

15. **A** ○ field   **B** ○ lunches   **C** ○ dollar

16. **A** ○ fire   **B** ○ ovens   **C** ○ class

17. **A** ○ foxes   **B** ○ puddle   **C** ○ sky

18. **A** ○ glasses   **B** ○ pond   **C** ○ flag

Choose the correct word to complete each sentence.

19. Where __ the ducks go?   **A** ○ does   **B** ○ do   **C** ○ fly

20. Do you wear __ watch?   **A** ○ a   **B** ○ an   **C** ○ two

21. The squirrel __ up into the tree.   **A** ○ ran   **B** ○ run   **C** ○ fast

22. The boy said __ would be back.   **A** ○ me   **B** ○ he   **C** ○ our

23. Our friends __ at school.   **A** ○ is   **B** ○ was   **C** ○ were

24. I was __ by the tree.   **A** ○ wait   **B** ○ waited   **C** ○ waiting

25. Dan and __ played catch.   **A** ○ me   **B** ○ I   **C** ○ him

26. Can Peter borrow __ ?   **A** ○ we   **B** ○ she   **C** ○ it

27. The band __ beautiful music.   **A** ○ play   **B** ○ played   **C** ○ playing

28. __ has a part in the play.   **A** ○ She   **B** ○ We   **C** ○ Me

29. Did you bring __ apple?   **A** ○ an   **B** ○ a   **C** ○ two

30. This orange is __ than that one.   **A** ○ sweet   **B** ○ sweeter   **C** ○ sweetest

31. You __ finished working.   **A** ○ is   **B** ○ are   **C** ○ was

32. I do not know who __ are.   **A** ○ I   **B** ○ he   **C** ○ they

33. I __ the dog last week.   **A** ○ sees   **B** ○ see   **C** ○ saw

34. Do __ need anything at the store?   **A** ○ me   **B** ○ we   **C** ○ us

35. They __ us now!   **A** ○ sees   **B** ○ see   **C** ○ saw

36. I hope that present is for __ .   **A** ○ I   **B** ○ me   **C** ○ they

37. He __ you his chair.   **A** ○ giving   **B** ○ give   **C** ○ gave

38. They __ nice friends.   **A** ○ have   **B** ○ has   **C** ○ do

39. He always __ me a smile.   **A** ○ gives   **B** ○ give   **C** ○ does

40. That is the __ frog I've ever seen! **A** ○ biggest   **B** ○ bigger   **C** ○ big

Writing Names of People

> ▪ Each word of a person's name begins with a **capital letter.**   EXAMPLE: **M**ary **A**nn **M**iller

▪ **Rewrite the names. Use capital letters where they are needed.**

1. mark twain Mark Twain _____

2. beverly cleary _____

3. diane dillon _____

4. lewis carroll _____

5. ezra jack keats _____

> ▪ Each word of a family name begins with a capital letter.   EXAMPLE: Here come **A**unt **A**nn and **G**randpa.

▪ **Circle the letters that should be capital letters.**

1. Today mother called grandma.

2. We will see grandma and grandpa at the party.

3. Will uncle carlos and aunt kathy be there, too?

▪ **Rewrite the sentences. Use capital letters where they are needed.**

1. Did dad help mom?

_____

2. grandma and I played ball.

_____

3. uncle frank is visiting us.

_____

Writing Initials

> ■ An **initial** stands for a person's name. It is a capital letter with a **period** (.) after it.
>   EXAMPLE: Steven Bell Mathis =
>   Steven **B.** Mathis or **S. B.** Mathis or **S. B. M.**

■ **Write the initials of each name.**

1. Robert Lawson ____R. L.____

5. Carol Frank _____

2. Carrie Anne Collier _____

6. Teresa Lynn Turner _____

3. Marcia Brown _____

7. Isaiah Bradley _____

4. Michael Bond _____

8. Lou Ann Walker _____

■ **Rewrite the names. Use initials for the names that are underlined.**

1. Joan Walsh Anglund

_____

3. Jane Yolen

_____

2. Lee Bennett Hopkins

_____

4. Patricia Ann Rosen

_____

■ **Rewrite the sentences. Be sure to write the initials correctly.**

TO:
Mrs. M. S. Mills
1907 Main St.
Saint Paul, MN
55155

1. The box was for m s mills.

_____

2. d e ellis sent it to her.

_____

3. t j lee brought the box to the house.

_____

Writing Titles of Respect

> - Begin a title of respect with a capital letter.
> - End <u>Mr.</u>, <u>Mrs.</u>, <u>Ms.</u>, and <u>Dr.</u> with a period. They are short forms, or **abbreviations,** of longer words.
>   EXAMPLES: **Mr.** George Selden   **Dr.** Alice Dahl
> - Do not end <u>Miss</u> with a period.

- **Rewrite the names correctly.**

1. mrs ruth scott _____

2. mr kurt wiese _____

3. miss e garcia _____

4. dr seuss _____

5. ms carol baylor _____

6. mr and mrs h cox _____

7. miss k e jones _____

- **Rewrite the sentences correctly.**

1. mrs h stone is here to see dr brooks.

   _____

2. dr brooks and ms miller are not here.

   _____

3. miss ari and mr lee came together.

   _____

4. mr f green will go in first.

   _____

Writing Names of Places

- Names of streets, parks, lakes, rivers, and schools
begin with a capital letter.
  EXAMPLES: **F**irst **S**treet
  Red **R**iver
  Central **P**ark

- **Rewrite the sentences. Use capital letters where they are needed.**

1. James lives on market street.

_____

2. I think thomas park is in this town.

_____

3. We went to mathis lake for a picnic.

_____

4. Is seton school far away?

_____

- The abbreviations of the words <u>street</u>, <u>road</u>, and
  <u>drive</u> in a place name begin with a capital letter
  and end with a period.
    EXAMPLES: Street = **St.** Main St.
    Road = **Rd.** Dove Rd.   Drive = **Dr.** East Dr.

- **Rewrite the place names. Use abbreviations.**

1. webb street Webb St.

4. hill road _____

2. airport road _____

5. bell street _____

3. doe drive _____

6. oak drive _____

Writing Names of Days

> - Names of days of the week begin with a capital letter.
>   EXAMPLES: **M**onday, **F**riday
> - The abbreviations of days of the week begin with a capital letter. They end with a period.
>   EXAMPLES: **S**un., **M**on., **T**ues., **W**ed., **T**hurs., **F**ri., **S**at.

Sunday	Monday	Tuesday	Wednesday	Thursday	Friday	Saturday
		1	2	3	4	5
6	7	8	9	10	11	12

- **Write the days to complete each sentence.**

   1. The first day of the week is _____.

   2. The day that comes before Saturday is _____.

   3. The day in the middle of the week is _____.

   4. Today is _____.

   5. I like _____ best.

- **Write the correct full name of each day. Then write the correct abbreviation.**

   1. sunday _____ Sunday _____ Sun.

   2. monday _____ _____

   3. tuesday _____ _____

   4. wednesday _____ _____

   5. thursday _____ _____

   6. friday _____ _____

   7. saturday _____ _____

Writing Names of Months

> - Names of the months begin with a capital letter.
> - The abbreviations of the months begin with a capital letter. They end with a period.
>   EXAMPLES: **J**an., **F**eb., **M**ar., **D**ec.

- **Write the months of the year correctly.**

  1. january _____

  2. february _____

  3. march _____

  4. april _____

  5. may _____

  6. june _____

  7. july _____

  8. august _____

  9. september _____

  10. october _____

  11. november _____

  12. december _____

- **Write the abbreviations of the months correctly.**

  1. jan _____   **4.** aug _____   **7.** oct _____

  2. mar _____   **5.** sept _____   **8.** dec _____

  3. nov _____   **6.** feb _____   **9.** apr _____

Writing Names of Seasons

> ▪ Names of the four seasons do not begin with capital letters.
>   EXAMPLES: **w**inter, **s**pring, **s**ummer, **f**all

winter	spring	summer	fall
December	March	June	September
January	April	July	October
February	May	August	November

▪ **Write the names of the four seasons on the top lines.
Then list the months under the season.**

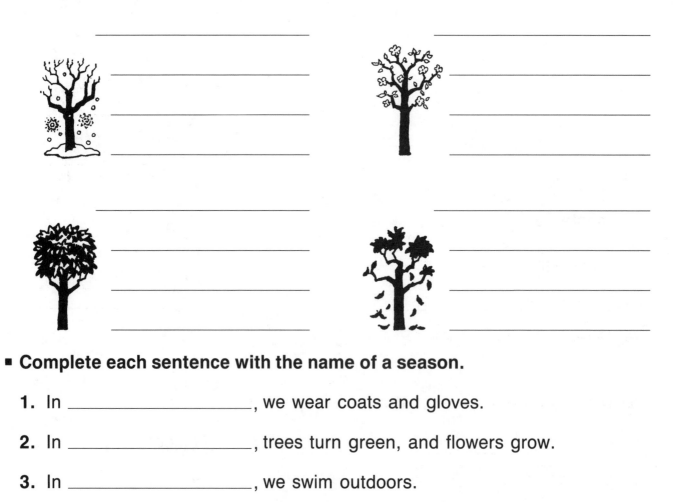

▪ **Complete each sentence with the name of a season.**

1. In _____, we wear coats and gloves.

2. In _____, trees turn green, and flowers grow.

3. In _____, we swim outdoors.

4. In _____, tree leaves turn red and yellow.

Writing Names of Holidays

> ■ Each word in the name of a holiday begins with a capital letter.   EXAMPLES: **V**alentine's **D**ay   **M**emorial **D**ay

■ **Write the holiday names correctly.**

1. new year's day _____

2. mother's day _____

3. independence day _____

4. labor day _____

5. victoria day _____

6. thanksgiving day _____

■ **Rewrite each sentence correctly.**

1. January 1 is new year's day.

   _____

2. I like valentine's day.

   _____

3. boxing day is a British holiday.

   _____

4. father's day is in June.

   _____

5. thanksgiving is on Thursday.

   _____

6. We have a picnic on independence day.

   _____

Writing Book Titles

- The first and last words in a book title begin with a capital letter.
- All other words begin with a capital letter except unimportant words. Some unimportant words are a, an, the, of, with, for, at, in, and on.

  EXAMPLES: **T**he **S**nowy **D**ay
  Storm at **S**ea

- **Write these book titles correctly.**

1. the doorbell rang

   _____

2. best friends

   _____

3. rabbits on roller skates

   _____

4. the cat in the hat

   _____

5. down on the sunny farm

   _____

6. fifty saves his friend

   _____

7. goodbye house

   _____

8. the biggest bear

   _____

Beginning Sentences

> ■ Begin a sentence with a capital letter.
> EXAMPLE: **N**ow Deb and Jet play together.

■ **Rewrite these sentences. Begin them with a capital letter.**

1. deb likes to play ball.

_____

2. her ball is red.

_____

3. jet wants to play.

_____

4. jet likes the ball.

_____

5. deb throws the ball.

_____

6. the ball goes far.

_____

7. jet runs to the ball.

_____

8. jet brings the ball back.

_____

9. deb hugs her dog.

_____

10. they have fun together.

_____

Ending Sentences

> ■ Put a **period** (.) at the end of a sentence that tells something.   EXAMPLE: Patty is my friend.

■ **Rewrite these telling sentences.**
Use capital letters and periods.

1. patty played on the baseball team

_____

2. she played hard

_____

3. she hit two home runs

_____

> ■ Put a **question mark** (?) at the end of a sentence that asks something.   EXAMPLE: Is he your brother?

■ **Rewrite these asking sentences.**
Use capital letters and question marks.

1. what time is it

_____

2. is it time for lunch

_____

3. are you ready to eat

_____

4. do you like apples

_____

Name _____   Date _____

Using Commas in Lists

- A **comma** (,) may take the place of the word <u>and</u> if a sentence lists three or more things. Keep the last <u>and</u>.
    EXAMPLE: We took pencils **and** paper **and** crayons **and** books to school. We took pencils, paper, crayons, **and** books to school.

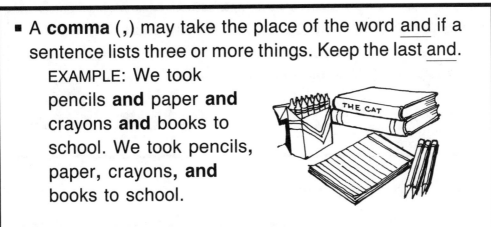

- **Put commas where they are needed.**

1. We go to school on Monday Tuesday Wednesday Thursday and Friday.

2. We draw sing and read on Monday.

3. Our class went to the post office the firehouse and the zoo.

4. We ran jumped laughed and ate at the zoo.

5. Elephants lions tigers and bears live at the zoo.

- **Rewrite the sentences. Use commas, and drop <u>and</u> where needed.**

1. Pam and Kay and Juan work hard.

   _____

2. Pam sings and dances and acts in the play.

   _____

3. Kay cleans and fixes and paints the stage.

   _____

Using Commas in Place Names

> - Names of cities and states begin with a capital letter.
> - Put a comma between the name of a city and its state.
>   EXAMPLES: Denver, Colorado
>   Dover, Delaware

- **Write the cities and states correctly.**

1. akron ohio _____ Akron, Ohio _____

2. hilo hawaii _____

3. macon georgia _____

4. nome alaska _____

5. provo utah _____

- **Rewrite the sentences. Use capital letters and commas where they are needed.**

1. Nancy lives in barnet vermont.

   _____

2. Mr. Hill went to houston texas.

   _____

3. Did Bruce like bend oregon?

   _____

4. Will Amy visit newark ohio?

   _____

5. How far away is salem maine?

   _____

Name _____   Date _____

Using Commas in Dates

> - Put a comma between the day of the month and
>   the year.   EXAMPLE: July 4, 1776

- **Write these dates correctly. Use capital letters,
  periods, and commas where they are needed.**

1. dec 12 1948 _____

2. mar 27 1965 _____

3. sept 8 1994 _____

4. nov 1 1999 _____

5. jan 5 1995 _____

- **Complete the sentences. Write the date correctly on the line.**

1. Jim was born on _____.
   (august 10 1967)

2. Jen's birthday is _____.
   (oct 17 1983)

3. Maria visited on _____.
   (february 8 1991)

4. Dad's party was on _____.
   (july 29 1989)

5. Carrie started school on _____.
   (sept 3 1991)

6. My library books go back on _____.
   (march 17 1998)

7. Luis lost his first tooth on _____.
   (oct 20 1988)

8. I was born on _____.

Using Apostrophes in Contractions

- A **contraction** is a word made by joining two words. An **apostrophe** (') shows where a letter or letters are left out.

  EXAMPLES: is not = isn't   can not = can't

               do not = don't   are not = aren't

- **Draw a line from the two words to the contraction.**

  1. were not   hasn't

  2. was not   haven't

  3. has not   wasn't

  4. have not   weren't

  5. did not   aren't

  6. are not   didn't

- **Write each contraction as two words.**

  1. isn't   is   not   5. didn't _____ _____

  2. don't _____ _____   6. hadn't _____ _____

  3. wasn't _____ _____   7. doesn't _____ _____

  4. can't _____ _____   8. aren't _____ _____

- **Write a contraction for the two words.**

  1. Today (is not) _____ a good day.

  2. I (do not) _____ have my lunch.

  3. I (did not) _____ finish my work.

  4. I (was not) _____ on time.

  5. My friends (were not) _____ on the bus.

Name _____   Date _____

Unit 5 Test

Choose the sentence with the correct capital letters.

1. **A** ○ Mrs. Fuller drove to Byrne Park.
   B ○ mrs. fuller drove to Byrne Park.
   C ○ Mrs. Fuller drove to byrne park.

2. **A** ○ aunt julie visited elm school.
   B ○ Aunt Julie visited Elm School.
   C ○ aunt Julie visited elm school.

3. **A** ○ Dr. A. Hanson is here.
   B ○ Dr. a. hanson is here.
   C ○ dr. A. Hanson is here.

4. **A** ○ next monday is a holiday.
   B ○ Next Monday is a holiday.
   C ○ Next monday is a Holiday.

5. **A** ○ School Starts in the Fall.
   B ○ school starts in the fall.
   C ○ School starts in the fall.

6. **A** ○ I made a card for Father's Day.
   B ○ i made a card for father's day.
   C ○ I made a card for father's Day.

7. **A** ○ It snowed last january.
   B ○ It snowed last January.
   C ○ it snowed last January.

8. **A** ○ Turn left on Fifth street.
   B ○ Turn left on fifth street.
   C ○ Turn left on Fifth Street.

9. **A** ○ Carlos flew to Austin, Texas.
   B ○ Carlos flew to austin, texas.
   C ○ carlos flew to Austin, Texas.

10. **A** ○ J. I. Ross met R. P. Cain.
    B ○ j. i. Ross met r. p. Cain.
    C ○ J. I. ross met R. P. cain.

Choose the book title with the correct capital letters.

11. **A** ○ Water life
    B ○ water life
    C ○ Water Life

12. **A** ○ Language Exercises
    B ○ language Exercises
    C ○ Language exercises

13. **A** ○ Voices from world history
    B ○ Voices from World History
    C ○ voices From world history

14. **A** ○ protecting wildlife
    B ○ Protecting Wildlife
    C ○ protecting Wildlife

Choose the correct short form for each word.

15. December   **A** ○ Decem.   **B** ○ Dec.   **C** ○ Dcbr.

16. cannot   **A** ○ cant'   **B** ○ can'ot   **C** ○ can't

17. Monday   **A** ○ Mond.   **B** ○ mo.   **C** ○ Mon.

18. Street   **A** ○ St.   **B** ○ Strt.   **C** ○ Str.

19. do not   **A** ○ don't   **B** ○ do'nt   **C** ○ d'ont

20. was not   **A** ○ wasn't   **B** ○ wasnt'   **C** ○ was'nt

21. have not   **A** ○ hav'nt   **B** ○ havnt'   **C** ○ haven't

22. Friday   **A** ○ Fr.   **B** ○ Fri.   **C** ○ fri

23. August   **A** ○ Agst.   **B** ○ Ag.   **C** ○ Aug.

24. Tuesday   **A** ○ Tues.   **B** ○ Tue   **C** ○ Tu.

25. are not   **A** ○ areno't   **B** ○ arn't   **C** ○ aren't

Choose the sentence with the correct periods, question marks, and commas.

26. A ○ Mr. J. Garcia was born on Oct 17 1965.
     B ○ Mr J Garcia was born on Oct. 17 1965.
     C ○ Mr. J. Garcia was born on Oct. 17, 1965.

27. A ○ Where was Dr. Blair on Apr. 12, 1989?
     B ○ Where was Dr. Blair on Apr. 12, 1989.
     C ○ Where was Dr Blair on Apr 12 1989?

28. A ○ Did you play on Dove St. last night.
     B ○ Did you play on Dove St last night?
     C ○ Did you play on Dove St. last night?

29. A ○ I will pack my clothes toys and books.
     B ○ I will pack my clothes, toys, and books.
     C ○ I will pack, my clothes, toys, and, books.

Name _____   Date _____

Writing Sentences

- Remember that **sentences** have a naming part and an action part.   EXAMPLE: Sarah won the race.

- **Draw a line from a naming part to an action part to make sentences.**

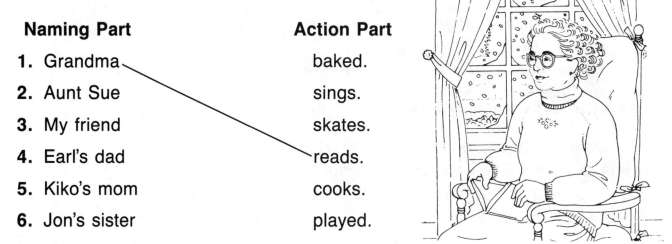

Naming Part	Action Part
1. Grandma	baked.
2. Aunt Sue	sings.
3. My friend	skates.
4. Earl's dad	reads.
5. Kiko's mom	cooks.
6. Jon's sister	played.

- **Write sentences with the naming parts and action parts you put together. Add some words of your own.**

1. Grandma reads by the window. _____

2. _____

3. _____

4. _____

5. _____

6. _____

- **Write a sentence about a friend.**

_____

_____

Name _____   Date _____

Paragraphs

- A **paragraph** is a group of sentences about one main idea.
- The first line of a paragraph is **indented.** There is a space before the first word.

  EXAMPLE:

      Fluffy is my cat. She is four years old. She is black and white. She likes to play with yarn. She likes napping in the sun.

- **Read the paragraphs. Answer the questions.**

    Charise is studying for her math test. The test is on Friday. She wants to get a good grade on the test. She knows that studying will help her do well on the test.

1. Who is this paragraph about? _____

2. Write the first sentence of the paragraph.

_____

    Today is my sister's birthday. She is five years old. She is having a party. Six of her friends are coming to the party. They will eat cake and play games.

1. What is this paragraph about? _____

_____

2. Write the first sentence of the paragraph. _____

_____

Name _____   Date _____

Main Idea

- The beginning sentence of a paragraph tells the **main idea.** It tells what the paragraph is about.
  EXAMPLE:
  I have nice neighbors. Ms. Hill gives me flowers. Mr. Stone always smiles and waves. Miss Higgins plays ball with me.

- **Read the paragraphs. Write the sentence that tells the main idea.**

Uncle Joe is a funny man. He tells jokes about elephants. He does magic tricks that don't work. He makes funny faces when he tells stories. He always makes me laugh.

1. _____

   _____

Dad told us a funny story about his dog. When Dad was a little boy, he had a dog named Tiger. One day Dad forgot his lunch. Dad said Tiger would bring it to school. A friend thought it would be a real tiger.

2. _____

   _____

Firefighters are brave people. They go into burning buildings. They put out fires. They teach families how to be safe in their homes.

3. _____

   _____

Name _____ Date _____

Supporting Details

> - The other sentences in a paragraph give **details** about the main idea in the beginning sentence.
>   EXAMPLE:
>   I have nice neighbors. **Ms. Hill gives me flowers. Mr. Stone always smiles and waves. Miss Higgins plays ball with me.**

- **Read the paragraphs. Circle the beginning sentences. Underline the sentences that give details about the main idea.**

Uncle Joe is a funny man. He tells jokes about elephants. He does magic tricks that don't work. He makes funny faces when he tells stories. He always makes me laugh.

Dad told us a funny story about his dog. When Dad was a little boy, he had a dog named Tiger. One day Dad forgot his lunch. Dad said Tiger would bring it to school. A friend thought it would be a real tiger.

Firefighters are brave people. They go into burning buildings. They put out fires. They teach families how to be safe in their homes.

Order in Paragraphs

- The sentences in a paragraph tell things in the order in which they happened.
- Words like <u>first</u>, <u>second</u>, <u>third</u>, <u>next</u>, <u>then</u>, and <u>last</u> can help tell when things happened.

  EXAMPLE:

  Jane got ready for bed. **First,** she took a bath. **Next,** she brushed her teeth. **Then** she put on her pajamas. **Last,** she read a story and got into bed.

- **Write 1, 2, 3, or 4 to show what happened first, second, third, and last.**

Eva planted flowers. First, she got a shovel. Next, she dug some holes in the garden. Then she put the flowers into the holes. Last, she put the shovel back in its place.

_____ Then she put the flowers into the holes.

_____ Next, she dug some holes in the garden.

_____ Last, she put the shovel back in its place.

_____ First, she got a shovel.

Dan and Larry washed the car. First, they got the car wet. Next, they put soap all over it. Then they washed all the soap off. Last, they dried the car.

_____ They put soap all over the car.

_____ They washed all the soap off.

_____ Dan and Larry dried the car.

_____ The boys got the car wet.

Parts of a Letter

- The **heading** of a letter tells where and when the letter was written.
- The **greeting** tells who will get the letter. The greeting begins with a capital letter and has a comma at the end. Each name in the greeting begins with a capital letter.
- The **body** tells what the letter is about.
- The **closing** says goodbye. There is a comma at the end. Only the first word of the closing begins with a capital letter.
- The **name** tells who wrote the letter.

608 Weston Dr.
Markham, Ontario L3R 1E5   } heading
Apr. 12, 19__

greeting ——→ Dear Chris,

   Our class went to the post office today. We
saw big bags of mail and busy workers.   } body
Then we saw many new stamps.
   Will you come to see me soon? I hope so.
                        Your friend, ←——— closing
                        Rose ←——— name

- **Read the sentences. Write the words.**

1. The letter is to _____.

2. The letter is from _____.

3. The letter writer lives at _____

_____.

Unit 6 Test

Read the paragraph. Answer the questions.

Saturday is the best day of the week for me. I can sleep later in the morning. I go shopping with my family. Sometimes I ride my bike to my friend's house.

1. Choose the sentence that gives the main idea.

A ○ Saturday is the best day of the week for me.

B ○ I can sleep later in the morning.

C ○ Sometimes I ride my bike to my friend's house.

2. Choose the sentence that gives a detail about the main idea.

A ○ Saturday is the best day of the week for me.

B ○ I can sleep later in the morning.

C ○ My brother likes Mondays.

Read the paragraph. Answer the questions.

Amy's old skates were too small. First, she saved all her birthday money. Next, she went shopping with her aunt. Then she bought new skates that fit.

3. Choose what happened first.

A ○ Amy bought new skates that fit.

B ○ Amy went shopping with her aunt.

C ○ Amy saved all her birthday money.

4. Choose what happened last.

A ○ Amy's old skates were too small.

B ○ Amy bought new skates that fit.

C ○ Amy saved all her birthday money.

Name _____   Date _____

Look at the letter. Choose the correct name for each numbered part of the letter.

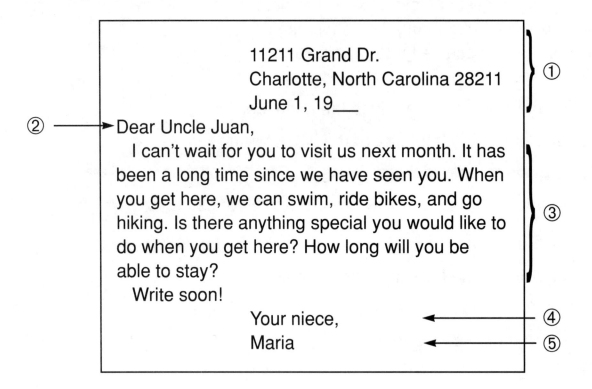

11211 Grand Dr.
Charlotte, North Carolina 28211
June 1, 19___   ①

② ──► Dear Uncle Juan,

    I can't wait for you to visit us next month. It has
been a long time since we have seen you. When
you get here, we can swim, ride bikes, and go
hiking. Is there anything special you would like to
do when you get here? How long will you be
able to stay?   ③
    Write soon!

                        Your niece,   ④
                        Maria   ⑤

5. What is part 1 of the letter called?

   A ○ closing   **B** ○ heading   **C** ○ body

6. What is part 4 of the letter called?

   A ○ heading   **B** ○ greeting   **C** ○ closing

7. What is part 5 of the letter called?

   A ○ name   **B** ○ closing   **C** ○ greeting

8. What is part 3 of the letter called?

   A ○ closing   **B** ○ heading   **C** ○ body

9. What is part 2 of the letter called?

   A ○ body   **B** ○ greeting   **C** ○ name

Answer Key

Assessment Test (Pages 8–11)

A. The following should be done:
  1. Put an X on the apple. **2.** Put an X to the right of the apple. **3.** Put an X above the apple. **4.** Draw a circle around the apple.

B. 1. east **2.** Shark Road **3.** south **4.** Dolphin Drive **5.** two

C. 1. pen **2.** name **3.** door

D. 1. Carol, Thomas, Zena **2.** carpet, door, window

E. 1. dear **2.** egg **3.** dust

F. 1. bill **2.** box **3.** to heat a liquid until bubbles form

G. 1. knew, pan **2.** angry, big **3.** short, narrow

H. 1. to **2.** hear **3.** there

I. The words in bold should be circled.
  1. A, **Who**, took **2.** X **3.** T, **I**, bought

J. The words in bold should be circled.
  1. Mr. Donaldson, grows **2.** plants, **April**

K. 1. were **2.** We **3.** a

L. The letters in bold should be circled, and punctuation marks should be added as shown.
  1. mr. **t. r. w**iggins and **i** went to **d**aytona **b**each last **s**aturday, **s**unday, and **m**onday. **2. r**honda went to the beach last **a**ugust. **3. d**idn't she take her cat named **w**hiskers?

M. The sentence in bold should be circled.
  Julia wanted to bake her friend a cake for his birthday. First, Julia read the recipe. Then she baked the cake. After the cake cooled, she put frosting on it.

N. 3, 2, 4, 1

Unit 1: Study Skills

Listening for Directions (P. 13)
Read the following directions to students:
1. Draw a doorknob on the door.
2. Draw a chimney on the roof.
3. Draw smoke coming out of the chimney.
4. Draw a window to the right of the door.
5. Draw a tree beside the left side of the house.
6. Draw a car in the driveway.

Check to see that students have correctly followed your directions.

More Listening for Directions (P. 14)
Read the following directions to students:
1. Your mother wants you to do a few things when you get home from school. These are her directions: First, make your bed. Then set the table. Finally, feed the cat.
2. Your friend invites you to come to his house. You have never been to his house before. Here are the directions he gives you: Go south on Red Road. Turn west on Green Street. Walk down two houses to 4202 Green Street.
3. Your teacher tells the class about a test. These are the directions: There will be a math test next Friday. It will be at 10:00. It will be on subtraction facts.
4. Your vet wants you to give your dog some medicine. Here are the directions: Give your dog one green pill in the morning. Give your dog a blue pill at noon. Give your dog another green pill in the evening.

Students should write the following key words:
1. 1) make your bed 2) set the table 3) feed the cat
2. 1) go south on Red Road 2) turn west on Green Street 3) walk down two houses to 4202
3. 1) math test next Friday 2) 10:00 3) on subtraction facts
4. 1) one green pill in the morning 2) a blue pill at noon 3) another green pill in the evening

Following Directions (P. 15)
Check to see that students mark an X in the following places:
1. above **2.** on **3.** under **4.** inside **5.** beside, left
6. beside, right

Following Written Directions (P. 16)
Check to see that students have colored the picture correctly.

Following Directions to a Place (P. 17)
1. south **2.** Fifth Avenue **3.** east **4.** Main Street **5.** 5

Making Comparisons (P. 18)
1. Robert **2.** Sara **3.** Robert **4.** Sara **5.** Robert
6. Sara **7.** Sara **8.** Robert **9.** Sara **10.** Robert

Organizing Information (P. 19)
Top: Students should cross out the following:
1. turtle **2.** dog **3.** elephant **4.** frog **5.** sister
6. popcorn **7.** candle **8.** mud **9.** cry **10.** blue

Bottom:

Colors	Names	Actions
red	Andy	eat
blue	Jenny	sing
yellow	Dennis	write
green	Lupe	dance
orange	Rudy	skip
pink	Vince	talk

Letters in ABC Order (P. 20)
Check students' work for all letters from E to Z.
1. U **2.** J **3.** D **4.** R **5.** O **6.** M **7.** X **8.** G **9.** Z **10.** Q
11. F **12.** L
1. K **2.** F **3.** R **4.** G **5.** X **6.** D **7.** U **8.** N **9.** T **10.** B
11. M **12.** E
1. A **2.** S **3.** M **4.** W **5.** I **6.** E **7.** K **8.** G **9.** P **10.** R
11. U **12.** J

Words in ABC Order (P. 21)
1. 2, 1, 3   air, bat, cat **2.** 3, 2, 1   rock, sea, top
3. 2, 3, 1   dog, egg, fish **4.** 2, 3, 1   gate, hat, ice
5. 1, 3, 2   joke, king, lake **6.** 2, 3, 1   mail, neck, owl
7. 3, 1, 2   us, very, well **8.** 2, 3, 1   X-ray, yes, zoo
9. 3, 2, 1   nail, oak, pan **10.** 1, 3, 2   quack, rug, sun

Finding Words in a Dictionary (P. 22)
Top: **1.** baby **2.** bed
Bottom: **1.** see / sit **2.** fit / fun **3.** race / run **4.** fit / fun
5. race / run **6.** see / sit

Using a Dictionary (P. 23)
1. middle **2.** paw **3.** open **4.** noise **5.** many
6. neighbor **7.** to go back **8.** never used before

Using a Dictionary (P. 24)
1. no **2.** yes **3.** no **4.** yes **5.** no **6.** yes **7.** yes **8.** no
9. no **10.** no

More Than One Meaning (P. 25)

Top: Students should circle the words in bold.

1. not warm

2. a sickness of the nose and throat

1. to fasten together with string

2. a cloth worn around the neck

1. moving water

2. to move the hands back and forth as a greeting

Bottom: **1.** tie, 1 **2.** tie, 2 **3.** wave, 1 **4.** wave, 2 **5.** cold, 1 **6.** cold, 2

Table of Contents (P. 26)

1. Pets **2.** 21 **3.** 7 **4.** 15 **5.** Fish **6.** Rabbits **7.** 7 **8.** 34 **9.** Dogs **10.** Birds

Unit 1 TEST, Pages 27–28

1. C **2.** A **3.** A **4.** C **5.** B **6.** C **7.** B **8.** C **9.** A **10.** B **11.** A **12.** C **13.** B **14.** A **15.** C **16.** C **17.** C **18.** A **19.** C **20.** B **21.** B **22.** C **23.** A **24.** C

Unit 2: Vocabulary

Words That Rhyme (P. 29)

Top: **1.** hop **2.** ring **3.** door **4.** dish **5.** ship **6.** duck
Bottom: **1.** coat **2.** rug **3.** tree **4.** box **5.** truck **6.** wig

Words That Mean the Same (P. 30)

1. road **2.** home **3.** sad **4.** sick **5.** gift **6.** small **7.** large **8.** dog **9.** yell **10.** great **11.** dad **12.** sleep

Words That Mean the Opposite (P. 31)

Top: **1.** soft **2.** long **3.** dark **4.** on **5.** happy **6.** low
Bottom: **1.** dry **2.** slow **3.** bad **4.** cold **5.** go **6.** hard **7.** dirty **8.** no

Words That Sound the Same (P. 32)

Top: **1.** hear **2.** here **3.** here **4.** hear **5.** here **6.** here
Bottom: **1.** their **2.** their **3.** there **4.** their **5.** there

More Words That Sound the Same (P. 33)

Top: **1.** write **2.** right **3.** right **4.** write **5.** right **6.** write **7.** write **8.** right **9.** right **10.** write **11.** right
Bottom: Sentences will vary.

Other Words That Sound the Same (P. 34)

1. to **2.** two **3.** to **4.** to **5.** too **6.** two **7.** too **8.** too **9.** to **10.** too **11.** to **12.** two **13.** too **14.** to

Words That Have Two Meanings (P. 35)

1. a **2.** b **3.** a **4.** a **5.** a **6.** b **7.** b **8.** a **9.** a **10.** a **11.** b **12.** a

Unit 2 TEST, Pages 36–37

1. A **2.** B **3.** C **4.** B **5.** C **6.** A **7.** A **8.** B **9.** C **10.** A **11.** B **12.** B **13.** A **14.** A **15.** B **16.** B **17.** A **18.** A **19.** B **20.** A

Unit 3: Sentences

Sentences (P. 38)

1. no **2.** yes **3.** no **4.** yes **5.** yes **6.** yes **7.** no **8.** no **9.** yes **10.** yes **11.** yes **12.** no **13.** yes **14.** no **15.** no **16.** yes

More Sentences (P. 39)

Top: **1.** Mrs. Brown lives on my street. **2.** Our building is made of wood. **3.** Four families live in our building. **4.** Our school went on a picnic. **5.** Jennifer was climbing the tree. **6.** The sun shone all day. **7.** Corn and beans grow on a farm. **8.** The wagon has a broken wheel. **9.** The mother goat fed the baby goat. **10.** The boat sailed in strong winds. **11.** The fisher caught seven fish. **12.** Some of the fish were sold in the store. **13.** Our team won ten games. **14.** Our batters hit the ball a lot. **15.** The ballpark was full of fans.

Bottom: Sentences will vary. Check for completeness.

Word Order in Sentences (P. 40)

1. My brother eats apples. **2.** Elizabeth drinks milk. **3.** Kim likes peanut butter. **4.** Justin wants bread. **5.** Chris plants corn. **6.** Chang caught a fish. **7.** Dad cooks breakfast. **8.** Shawn shares his lunch. **9.** Rosa grew the carrot. **10.** Kate looks at the pie.

Telling Sentences (P. 41)

The following sentences are telling sentences:
1, 2, 4, 5, 7, 8, 10, 12, 14, 15

Asking Sentences (P. 42)

The following sentences are asking sentences:
1, 2, 4, 6, 7, 9, 10, 11, 13, 15

Kinds of Sentences (P. 43)

Top: **1.** asking **2.** telling **3.** asking **4.** telling **5.** telling **6.** asking **7.** telling **8.** telling **9.** asking **10.** asking
Bottom:

Telling Sentences	Asking Sentences
I went to the toy store.	Which toy do you want?
I picked a game.	Are there any puzzles?

Naming Part of Sentences (P. 44)

Students should circle the following parts of each sentence:
1. My family and I **2.** Sally Harper **3.** Miss Jenkins **4.** Mr. Olson **5.** Henry **6.** Mr. Byrne **7.** Mrs. Lee **8.** Mr. and Mrs. Diaz **9.** Jeanine **10.** Mr. Wolf **11.** Sammy Taft **12.** Mr. O'Dowd **13.** Nina **14.** Some children **15.** Mrs. Clark **16.** Carolyn and Albert **17.** Julie

Action Part of Sentences (P. 45)

Students should circle the following parts of each sentence:
1. live on a busy street **2.** found a bird **3.** drives very slowly **4.** walks his dog **5.** throws to his dog **6.** cuts his grass **7.** picks up her children **8.** shop for food **9.** plays in the park **10.** brings the mail **11.** brings the paper **12.** cooks dinner **13.** paints the house **14.** plant a garden **15.** washes her windows **16.** plant flower seeds **17.** waters the garden

Sentence Parts (P. 46)

Top: **1.** Lions **2.** Zebras **3.** A pig **4.** A cat **5.** My dog **6.** Fish **7.** Birds
Middle: **1.** fly **2.** buzz **3.** barks **4.** quack **5.** hops **6.** roar **7.** moo
Bottom: Sentences will vary.

Unit 3 TEST, Pages 47–48

1. B **2.** A **3.** B **4.** A **5.** B **6.** B **7.** A **8.** A **9.** B **10.** A **11.** B **12.** B **13.** C **14.** B **15.** A **16.** A **17.** B **18.** C **19.** A **20.** A **21.** B **22.** A **23.** B **24.** A **25.** B **26.** A **27.** A **28.** B **29.** B **30.** A **31.** B **32.** B **33.** A **34.** B **35.** B **36.** A

Unit 4: Grammar and Usage

Naming Words (P. 49)

Top: **1.** apple **2.** bird **3.** boy **4.** car **5.** chair **6.** desk **7.** girl **8.** grass **9.** pen **10.** rug **11.** tree **12.** truck
Bottom:

1. The <u>girl</u> eats an <u>apple</u>.	girl, apple
2. A <u>bird</u> flies to the <u>tree</u>.	bird, tree
3. A <u>chair</u> is by the <u>desk</u>.	chair, desk
4. A <u>boy</u> sits in the <u>chair</u>.	boy, chair
5. The <u>girl</u> plays with a <u>truck</u>.	girl, truck
6. The <u>truck</u> is on the <u>rug</u>.	truck, rug

Special Naming Words (P. 50)
Top: **1.** Bob's Bikes **2.** Bridge Road **3.** China **4.** Elf
Corn **5.** Gabriel **6.** Linda **7.** New York City **8.** Ohio
9. Pat Green **10.** State Street
Bottom:
1. I bought apples at Hill's Store.   Hill's Store
2. The store is on Baker Street.   Baker Street
3. It is near Stone Library.   Stone Library
4. I gave an apple to Emily Fuller.   Emily Fuller

One and More Than One (P. 51)
Top: **1.** caps **2.** chairs **3.** girls **4.** trees **5.** flags **6.** boys
Middle: **1.** lunches **2.** dresses **3.** glasses **4.** dishes
5. boxes **6.** watches
Bottom: **1.** ponds **2.** pigs **3.** brushes **4.** frogs
5. wishes **6.** benches **7.** axes **8.** balls

Action Words (P. 52)
Top: **1.** The boy reads. **2.** The baby cries. **3.** The rabbit
hops. **4.** The birds sing. **5.** The dogs bark.
Bottom: **1.** runs **2.** kicks **3.** breaks **4.** looks **5.** shakes
6. turns **7.** runs **8.** talks **9.** sends **10.** talks **11.** pays
12. shakes **13.** plays

Naming Word or Action Word (P. 53)
1. class, room **2.** teacher, stories **3.** stories, elephants
4. Elephants, animals
Middle: **1.** takes **2.** put **3.** rub **4.** wash **5.** pour
Bottom: **1.** verb **2.** noun **3.** noun **4.** verb **5.** noun
6. verb **7.** noun **8.** verb **9.** noun

Adding -ed or -ing to Verbs (P. 54)
Top: **1.** played **2.** called **3.** wanted **4.** laughed
5. jumped **6.** played **7.** laughing **8.** playing
9. watching **10.** talking
Bottom: **1.** Carmen is finishing her work now. **2.** Carmen
helped Grandma cook yesterday. **3.** Grandma is cooking
some soup today.

Using Is or Are (P. 55)
Top: **1.** are **2.** is **3.** are **4.** is **5.** are **6.** are **7.** are
8. is **9.** are
Bottom: Sentences will vary.

Using Was or Were (P. 56)
Top: **1.** were **2.** was **3.** were **4.** were **5.** were **6.** was
7. was **8.** were **9.** was
Bottom: Sentences will vary.

Using See, Sees, or Saw (P. 57)
Top: **1.** sees **2.** saw **3.** sees **4.** sees **5.** saw **6.** saw
7. see **8.** saw **9.** saw **10.** see
Bottom:
1. saw   Last week we saw Lee.
2. sees   Lee sees my painting now.

Using Run, Runs, or Ran (P. 58)
1. ran   Horses ran wild long ago.
2. run   A horse can run ten miles every day.
3. run   Can you run as fast as a horse?
4. ran   Mandy ran in a race last week.
5. runs   Andy runs home from school now.
6. runs   Now Mandy runs after Andy.
7. run   How far can you run?

Using Give, Gives, or Gave (P. 59)
Top: **1.** give **2.** gave **3.** gives **4.** gave **5.** gave **6.** gave
7. gave **8.** gave **9.** gives **10.** give
Bottom: Sentences will vary.

Using Do or Does (P. 60)
Top: **1.** do **2.** does **3.** does **4.** does **5.** does **6.** do
7. does **8.** do **9.** does **10.** do **11.** do **12.** do
Bottom: Sentences will vary.

Using Has, Have, or Had (P. 61)
1. had **2.** has **3.** have **4.** have **5.** has **6.** had **7.** has
8. has **9.** have **10.** had **11.** had **12.** has **13.** had
14. had

Pronouns (P. 62)
1. She got a gift. **2.** It was for her birthday.
3. He brought the gift. **4.** They found a box.
5. We are going to the party. **6.** They will wear hats.
7. She likes punch. **8.** It will end soon.

Using I or Me (P. 63)
Top: **1.** I **2.** I **3.** me **4.** me **5.** I **6.** I
Bottom: **1.** I **2.** me **3.** I **4.** I **5.** I **6.** me **7.** I **8.** I

Using A or An (P. 64)
1. an **2.** a **3.** a **4.** an **5.** a **6.** an **7.** an **8.** an **9.** a
10. a **11.** a **12.** a **13.** an **14.** an **15.** a **16.** a **17.** a
18. an **19.** an **20.** a **21.** an **22.** an **23.** an **24.** a

Using Words That Compare (P. 65)
1. younger   Dad is younger than Mom.
2. oldest   Kim is the oldest of four children.
3. smaller   An ant is smaller than a pig.
4. longest   That snake is the longest of the six at the zoo.
5. taller   The barn is taller than the house.
6. stronger   Alex is stronger than Michael.
7. softest   That blue chair is the softest in the room.

Unit 4 TEST, Pages 66–67
1. A **2.** B **3.** A **4.** A **5.** A **6.** B **7.** A **8.** B **9.** A **10.** A
11. B **12.** A **13.** C **14.** A **15.** B **16.** B **17.** A **18.** A
19. B **20.** A **21.** A **22.** B **23.** C **24.** C **25.** B **26.** C
27. B **28.** A **29.** A **30.** B **31.** B **32.** C **33.** C **34.** B
35. B **36.** B **37.** C **38.** A **39.** A **40.** A

Unit 5: Capitalization and Punctuation

Writing Names of People (P. 68)
Top: **1.** Mark Twain **2.** Beverly Cleary **3.** Diane Dillon
4. Lewis Carroll **5.** Ezra Jack Keats
Middle: Students should circle the first letter of the
following: **1.** mother, grandma **2.** grandma, grandpa
3. uncle carlos, aunt kathy
Bottom: **1.** Did Dad help Mom? **2.** Grandma and I played
ball. **3.** Uncle Frank is visiting us.

Writing Initials (P. 69)
Top: **1.** R. L. **2.** C. A. C. **3.** M. B. **4.** M. B. **5.** C. F.
6. T. L. T. **7.** I. B. **8.** L. A. W.
Middle: **1.** J. W. A. **2.** L. B. Hopkins **3.** J. Yolen
4. P. A. R.
Bottom: **1.** The box was for M. S. Mills. **2.** D. E. Ellis sent
it to her. **3.** T. J. Lee brought the box to the house.

Writing Titles of Respect (P. 70)
Top: **1.** Mrs. Ruth Scott **2.** Mr. Kurt Wiese **3.** Miss E.
Garcia **4.** Dr. Seuss **5.** Ms. Carol Baylor **6.** Mr. and Mrs.
H. Cox **7.** Miss K. E. Jones
Bottom: **1.** Mrs. H. Stone is here to see Dr. Brooks. **2.** Dr.
Brooks and Ms. Miller are not here. **3.** Miss Ari and Mr.
Lee came together. **4.** Mr. F. Green will go in first.

Writing Names of Places (P. 71)

Top: **1.** James lives on Market Street. **2.** I think Thomas Park is in this town. **3.** We went to Mathis Lake for a picnic. **4.** Is Seton School far away?

Bottom: **1.** Webb St. **2.** Airport Rd. **3.** Doe Dr. **4.** Hill Rd. **5.** Bell St. **6.** Oak Dr.

Writing Names of Days (P. 72)

Top: **1.** Sunday **2.** Friday **3.** Wednesday **4.-5.** Answers will vary.

Bottom: **1.** Sunday, Sun. **2.** Monday, Mon. **3.** Tuesday, Tues. **4.** Wednesday, Wed. **5.** Thursday, Thurs. **6.** Friday, Fri. **7.** Saturday, Sat.

Writing Names of Months (P. 73)

Top: **1.** January **2.** February **3.** March **4.** April **5.** May **6.** June **7.** July **8.** August **9.** September **10.** October **11.** November **12.** December

Bottom: **1.** Jan. **2.** Mar. **3.** Nov. **4.** Aug. **5.** Sept. **6.** Feb. **7.** Oct. **8.** Dec. **9.** Apr.

Writing Names of Seasons (P. 74)

Top:

winter	spring	summer	fall
December	March	June	September
January	April	July	October
February	May	August	November

Bottom: **1.** winter **2.** spring **3.** summer **4.** fall

Writing Names of Holidays (P. 75)

Top: **1.** New Year's Day **2.** Mother's Day **3.** Independence Day **4.** Labor Day **5.** Victoria Day **6.** Thanksgiving Day

Bottom: **1.** January 1 is New Year's Day. **2.** I like Valentine's Day. **3.** Boxing Day is a British holiday. **4.** Father's Day is in June. **5.** Thanksgiving is on Thursday. **6.** We have a picnic on Independence Day.

Writing Book Titles (P. 76)

1. The Doorbell Rang **2.** Best Friends **3.** Rabbits on Roller Skates **4.** The Cat in the Hat **5.** Down on the Sunny Farm **6.** Fifty Saves His Friend **7.** Goodbye House **8.** The Biggest Bear

Beginning Sentences (P. 77)

1. Deb likes to play ball. **2.** Her ball is red. **3.** Jet wants to play. **4.** Jet likes the ball. **5.** Deb throws the ball. **6.** The ball goes far. **7.** Jet runs to the ball **8.** Jet brings the ball back. **9.** Deb hugs her dog. **10.** They have fun together.

Ending Sentences (P. 78)

Top: **1.** Patty played on the baseball team. **2.** She played hard. **3.** She hit two home runs.

Bottom: **1.** What time is it? **2.** Is it time for lunch? **3.** Are you ready to eat? **4.** Do you like apples?

Using Commas in Lists (P. 79)

Top: **1.** We go to school on Monday, Tuesday, Wednesday, Thursday, and Friday. **2.** We draw, sing, and read on Monday. **3.** Our class went to the post office, the firehouse, and the zoo. **4.** We ran, jumped, laughed, and ate at the zoo. **5.** Elephants, lions, tigers, and bears live at the zoo.

Bottom: **1.** Pam, Kay, and Juan work hard. **2.** Pam sings, dances, and acts in the play. **3.** Kay cleans, fixes, and paints the stage.

Using Commas in Place Names (P. 80)

Top: **1.** Akron, Ohio **2.** Hilo, Hawaii **3.** Macon, Georgia **4.** Nome, Alaska **5.** Provo, Utah

Bottom: **1.** Nancy lives in Barnet, Vermont. **2.** Mr. Hill went to Houston, Texas. **3.** Did Bruce like Bend, Oregon? **4.** Will Amy visit Newark, Ohio? **5.** How far away is Salem, Maine?

Using Commas in Dates (P. 81)

Top: **1.** Dec. 12, 1948 **2.** Mar. 27, 1965 **3.** Sept. 8, 1994 **4.** Nov. 1, 1999 **5.** Jan. 5, 1995

Bottom: **1.** Jim was born on August 10, 1967. **2.** Jen's birthday is Oct. 17, 1983. **3.** Maria visited on February 8, 1991. **4.** Dad's party was on July 29, 1989. **5.** Carrie started school on Sept. 3, 1991. **6.** My library books go back on March 17, 1998. **7.** Luis lost his first tooth on Oct. 20, 1988. **8.** Answers will vary.

Using Apostrophes in Contractions (P. 82)

Top: **1.** were not, weren't **2.** was not, wasn't **3.** has not, hasn't **4.** have not, haven't **5.** did not, didn't **6.** are not, aren't

Middle: **1.** is not **2.** do not **3.** was not **4.** can not **5.** did not **6.** had not **7.** does not **8.** are not

Bottom: **1.** isn't **2.** don't **3.** didn't **4.** wasn't **5.** weren't

Unit 5 TEST, Pages 83–84

1. A **2.** B **3.** A **4.** B **5.** C **6.** A **7.** B **8.** C **9.** A **10.** A **11.** C **12.** A **13.** B **14.** B **15.** B **16.** C **17.** C **18.** A **19.** A **20.** A **21.** C **22.** B **23.** C **24.** A **25.** C **26.** C **27.** A **28.** C **29.** B

Unit 6: Composition

Writing Sentences (P. 85)

Top, Middle, and Bottom: Sentences will vary.

Paragraphs (P. 86)

Top: **1.** Charise **2.** Charise is studying for her math test.

Bottom: **1.** My sister's birthday **2.** Today is my sister's birthday.

Main Idea (P. 87)

1. Uncle Joe is a funny man. **2.** Dad told us a funny story about his dog. **3.** Firefighters are brave people.

Supporting Details (P. 88)

Students should circle the first sentence in each paragraph and underline all the other sentences.

Order in Paragraphs (P. 89)

Top: 3, 2, 4, 1 Bottom: 2, 3, 4, 1

Parts of a Letter (P. 90)

Tell students to fill in the current year.

1. Chris **2.** Rose **3.** 608 Weston Dr., Markham, Ontario L3R 1E5

Unit 6 TEST, Pages 91–92

1. A **2.** B **3.** C **4.** B **5.** B **6.** C **7.** A **8.** C **9.** B